D0474030

GREAT TASTES

QUICK SHORT RECIPES

First published in 2010 by Bay Books, an imprint of Murdoch Books Pty Limited
This edition published in 2010.

Murdoch Books Australia
Pier 8/9
23 Hickson Road
Millers Point NSW 2000
Phone: +61 (0) 2 8220 2000
Fax: +61 (0) 2 8220 2558
www.murdochbooks.com.au

Murdoch Books UK Limited
Erico House, 6th Floor
93–99 Upper Richmond Road
Putney, London SW15 2TG
Phone: +44 (0) 20 8785 5995
Fax: +44 (0) 20 8785 5985
www.murdochbooks.co.uk

Chief Executive: Juliet Rogers
Publishing Director: Kay Scarlett
Publisher: Lynn Lewis
Senior Designer: Heather Menzies
Designer: Melanie Young
Production: Kita George
Index: Jo Rudd

© Text, design and photography copyright Murdoch Books 2010.
All rights reserved. No part of this publication may be reproduced, stored in a retrieval system or transmitted in any form or by any means, electronic, mechanical, photocopying, recording or otherwise, without the prior written permission of the publisher.

ISBN: 9780681690837

PRINTED IN CHINA

OVEN GUIDE: You may find cooking times vary depending on the oven you are using. For fan-forced ovens, as a general rule, set the oven temperature to 20°C (35°F) lower than indicated in the recipe.

GREAT TASTES

QUICK SHORT RECIPES

More than 120 easy recipes for every day

bay books

CONTENTS

QUICK COOKING BASICS...6

STARTERS AND SNACKS..8

MAINS...44

SALADS..90

DESSERTS..134

INDEX...158

QUICK COOKING BASICS

It's always a big help to have a fund of good recipes to turn to when you're in a hurry. Creating a meal and sitting down to enjoy it should be pleasurable activities, and the more help we can all get, the better! This compilation of recipes was created with today's busy cooks in mind.

Where possible, the recipes feature short lists of ingredients and many items are readily available at your local supermarket. And, they can be prepared quickly. One thing they're definitely not short on, however, is flavour. Occasionally, more unusual and exotic ingredients are included, reflecting our growing interest in flavours and cooking styles from around the world. However, with the proliferation of Japanese, Middle Eastern and Asian food shops, good-quality delicatessens and specialty goods' sections in the larger supermarket chains, finding these ingredients is no longer the difficult task it once was.

Get organised

Family meals are a test of organisational skill. And, even cooking for one or two people can be a challenge when you're time poor and feeling tired. First, you need to decide what to prepare. Be realistic about the recipes you choose for the week ahead and don't commit yourself to anything that may require more of your time than you have available. Then the pantry has to be checked for ingredients and any essential shopping must be done. Finally, there's the preparation and serving of the food.

Minimising preparation time does not mean compromising on nutritional value, quality of ingredients or the final product. It just means being organised so that you'll have more of that precious leisure time.

Remember that fresh ingredients, when available, are always preferable to dried, canned or frozen foods. Use your discretion when shopping. In most cases, fresh ingredients don't take very much longer to prepare than the so-called 'convenience' item. If, on the other hand, you want to cook a recipe that includes vegetables such as spinach or peas that are out of season, the frozen or canned varieties will be acceptable. Never buy wilted or stale vegetables—choose a substitute. Even if you have only the smallest of backyards or just a balcony, try growing some vegetables for yourself in the ground or in tubs. It's a very rewarding thing to do. Spinach, cherry tomatoes and lettuces need very little room to grow and not too much maintenance.

Stocking the pantry

Stocking your pantry with the basics will prove invaluable in getting great meals on the table with minimum fuss. We've made suggestions here for the pantry contents, but your own pantry will reflect the tastes and preferences of you and your family. Check the contents often and make sure frequently used items are replenished before they run out. In the case of canned goods that keep for a long time, stock up on your favourite brands when you see them 'on special'. Follow these suggestions and you will always have the beginnings of a nutritious, flavour-packed meal on hand.

Staples should include flours, sugars, salt, pepper, rice and pasta. As well, keep a good supply of pasta sauces, cans of tomatoes and tomato passata, as well as packs of ready-made chicken, beef and vegetable stock.

Buy good quality olive oil and other cooking oils such as peanut and safflower, as well as different kinds of vinegar.

Dried herbs and spices are very useful. Check the use-by date on both on a regular basis. It's very easy to forget how long you have had them. Once the fragrance, flavour and colour start to fade, no matter what the use-by date, it's best to discard the product. It won't enhance your cooking if it has deteriorated.

For quick curry-making, you'll need Thai sweet chilli sauce, soy sauce, ready-made curry pastes, and sambal oelek (a mixture of chopped chilli and salt). If you love Japanese food, stock up on mirin, rice wine vinegar, dried soba noodles and other staples. Some condiments need to be refrigerated after opening—just follow the instructions on the bottles.

And, always have plenty of onions, potatoes, garlic and ginger to hand and store them in a cool, dry place.

Store your supplies in a cool, dry place.

Stock up on jars of condiments, pasta and rice.

Use day-old bread to make breadcrumbs for coatings..

Process the bread until the crumbs are the size you need.

Other necessities include refrigerated items such as butter, milk, eggs and cheeses. For the freezer, stock up on pizza bases, different types of pastry and wrappers for making spring rolls. Frozen peas and broad beans are useful, too.

Purchase and storage

Onions Always have a selection on hand. Choose firm onions with dry, papery skins; avoid sprouting specimens or any that feel spongy. Onions should be stored in a cool, dry, dark place, or refrigerated. To spare your eyes brimming with tears when you prepare them, place onions in the freezer for 15 minutes, or refrigerate for about an hour, before peeling and chopping.

Brown onions have a stronger flavour than white, will store well and are excellent for making casseroles and soups. White onions are milder in flavour and do not store as well. Use them raw in salads.

Red onions have a relatively mild, slightly sweet taste and can also be used raw in salads.

Potatoes There is an astonishing variety of potatoes available these days, some waxy, some floury, some all-purpose. Many varieties come in bags on the front of which is information on what they are best used for. Buy a few different varieties and experiment to find out what works and tastes best for you. Look for kipfler, ruby rose, pontiac, coliban, desiree and many more.

Avoid soft or spongy potatoes and ones that are discoloured or bruised. Don't buy any that are starting to sprout, as these have been stored for too long. If there are any greenish spots, cut them out, but if the whole potato is green, discard it as it can be toxic. Keep potatoes in a cool, dark, dry place. If stored correctly, they will keep for several weeks. Avoid refrigeration and remove them from plastic bags as they will cause softening and sprouting to occur.

Herbs Buy fresh whenever possible. Better still, grow some of your own on a window sill or in your backyard. If you use dried, generally you will need a third the quantity given for fresh.

Cook ahead

When you do have some spare time, it's well worth doing as much preparation ahead as possible. Read your chosen recipe carefully and see what elements of it you can tackle early on. Cook a sauce for the meat dish so all you have to do is add it when needed (and make a double quantity so you can freeze some for another meal).

It's always a good idea to cook in bulk and freeze the leftovers for another time. Items such as crepes can be made in bulk and then frozen, separated between layers of baking paper. Peel off the number you want as and when you need and reheat gently. Ice creams and sorbets made from a glut of seasonal fruit are fun to make and are impressive 'instant' desserts. Plain madeira and sponge cakes can be baked, sliced and frozen well ahead and then quickly defrosted and dressed up with simple sauces and custards.

At the end of the day, choose what works best for you and your circumstances. Remember, using convenience products isn't something to feel guilty about. While it's a pleasure to make your own pesto from scratch when you have the time and inclination, the world is not going to come to an end if you resort to one of the many good-quality ready-made pesto mixtures on sale in supermarkets when necessary. All things in moderation. Be kind to yourself and enjoy cooking!

Flatten garlic with the back of a knife and the skin will peel away quickly and easily.

Whole tinned tomatoes can be chopped in the tin with kitchen scissors to save time.

Beans and pulses can be prepared overnight.

Freeze scoops of tomato paste (concentrated purée) in ice-cube trays for later use.

STARTERS & SNACKS

CHEESE AND CHILLI SHAPES

MAKES 26

150 g (5½ oz/1¼ cups) plain (all-purpose) flour

pinch of dry hot mustard

90 g (3 oz) tablespoons butter, roughly chopped

60 g (2 oz/½ cup) grated vintage cheddar cheese

4 red chillies, seeded and sliced

1 egg yolk

1   Process the flour, mustard and butter until they resemble fine breadcrumbs. Add cheese and chilli, then the egg yolk and 1 tablespoon water. Process until the mixture comes together. Gather into a ball, cover with plastic wrap and refrigerate for 30 minutes.

2   Preheat oven to 190°C (375°F/Gas 5). On a lightly floured surface, roll out the dough to a 5 mm (¼ inch) thickness. Cut into 5 cm (2 inch) rounds.

3   Place on lightly greased baking tray and bake for about 18 minutes, or until golden. Cool.

TZATZIKI

SERVES 12

2 Lebanese (short) cucumbers

400 g (14 oz/1⅔ cups) low-fat plain
yoghurt

4 garlic cloves, crushed

3 tablespoons finely chopped mint, plus
extra, to garnish

1 tablespoon lemon juice

1 **Cut the cucumbers** in half lengthways, scoop out the seeds and discard. Leave the skin on and coarsely grate the cucumber into a small colander. Sprinkle with salt and leave over a large bowl for 15 minutes to drain off any bitter juices.

2 **Meanwhile, stir together** the yoghurt, garlic, mint and lemon juice.

3 **Rinse the cucumber** under cold water then, taking small handfuls, squeeze out any excess moisture. Combine the grated cucumber with the yoghurt mixture and season well with salt and freshly ground black pepper. Garnish with mint. Serve with vegetable crudités (see Notes).

Notes: Tzatziki will keep in an airtight container in the fridge for 2–3 days.

To make vegetable crudités, cut raw carrots, celery, zucchini (courgettes) and unpeeled Lebanese (short) cucumbers into 7.5 cm (3 inch) sticks and raw cauliflower and broccoli into small florets.

TAPENADE

SERVES 10

400 g (14 oz/2⅔ cups) pitted kalamata olives

2 garlic cloves, crushed

2 anchovy fillets in oil, drained

2 tablespoons capers in brine, rinsed and squeezed dry

2 teaspoons chopped thyme leaves

2 teaspoons dijon mustard

1 tablespoon lemon juice

3 tablespoons olive oil

1 tablespoon brandy (optional)

1 Place kalamata olives, crushed garlic, anchovies, capers, chopped thyme, dijon mustard, lemon juice, oil and brandy in a food processor and process until smooth. Season to taste with salt and freshly ground black pepper. Spoon into a clean, warm jar, cover with a layer of olive oil, seal and refrigerate for up to 1 week. Serve on bruschetta or with a mixed plate of cold meats, pickled vegetables and breads.

Note: To make sure your storage jar is very clean, preheat the oven to 120°C (250°F/Gas ½). Wash the jar and lid thoroughly in hot soapy water (or preferably in a dishwasher) and rinse well with hot water. Put the jar on a baking tray and place in the oven for 20 minutes, or until fully dry and you are ready to use it. Do not dry the jar or lid with a tea towel (dish towel).

GREAT TASTES QUICK SHORT RECIPES

BRUSCHETTA

MAKES 8

4 roma (plum) tomatoes, chopped

4 tablespoons olive oil

1 tablespoon balsamic vinegar

2 tablespoons chopped basil, plus extra, to garnish

8 slices day-old crusty Italian bread

1 garlic clove, peeled

1 **Combine the tomatoes,** olive oil, balsamic vinegar and chopped basil. Season well.

2 **Toast the bread** on one side. Rub the toasted side lightly with a peeled clove of garlic. Top with the tomato mixture and garnish with the extra chopped basil. Serve immediately.

CRUNCHY CHEESE BITES

MAKES ABOUT 20

250 g (9 oz/2 cups) grated cheddar cheese

125 g (4½ oz) feta cheese, crumbled

3 tablespoons ricotta cheese

3 tablespoons chopped spring onions (scallions)

1 small tomato, chopped

1 egg, beaten

4 sheets ready-rolled puff pastry

beaten egg, to brush

milk, to brush

1 **Preheat the oven** to 220°C (425°F/Gas 7). Combine the cheeses, spring onion, tomato and egg in a bowl. Season with freshly ground black pepper.

2 **Cut the pastry** into rounds using a 10 cm (4 inch) cutter. Place heaped teaspoons of mixture on one half of each round.

3 **Fold the pastry** over filling to make semi-circles, brush the edges between the pastry with a little of the beaten egg and press the edges together firmly with a fork to seal.

4 **Place on a baking tray** and brush with a little milk. Bake in the oven for 10–15 minutes, or until puffed and golden. Allow the pastries to cool for at least 10 minutes before serving

VEGETABLE STRUDELS

MAKES 16

165 g (6 oz/1 heaped cup) potato flour

265 g (9 oz/1½ cups) rice flour

3 teaspoons baking powder

125 g (4½ oz) butter

canola oil, for deep-frying

VEGETABLE FILLING

2 teaspoons butter

2 tablespoons oil

1 garlic clove, crushed

300 g (10½ oz) potatoes, peeled, chopped and partly cooked

150 g (5½ oz/1 cup) swede (rutabaga), cubed and partly cooked

60 g (2 oz/½ cup) chopped green beans

3 spring onions (scallions), thinly sliced

1 Sift the dry ingredients into a bowl. Rub the butter in with your fingertips until the mixture resembles fine breadcrumbs. Make a well in the centre. Add enough water to make a soft dough. Turn onto a floured board and knead lightly. Divide dough into four equal portions. Roll each portion out into a 32 cm (12½ inch) square, 5 mm (¼ inch) thick, between two sheets of baking paper. Cut each square into four squares—you should have 16 squares in all.

2 For the vegetable filling, put the butter and oil into a saucepan. Heat over medium heat until butter melts. Add the garlic, vegetables and spring onions and mix well. Cook, covered, over low heat for 6 minutes, or until the vegetables are tender. Set aside to cool completely (if the filling is warm, it will soften and split the dough).

3 Divide the filling evenly among the dough squares. Brush the edges with water and fold the corners over to envelop the filling.

4 Fill a large saucepan or deep-fat fryer one-third full with oil and heat to 180°C (350°F), or until a cube of bread dropped into the oil browns in 15 seconds. Deep-fry the strudels in small batches. Drain on paper towels. Keep hot in a warm oven until all are cooked. Serve hot.

PRAWN COCKTAILS

SERVES 6

COCKTAIL SAUCE

250 g (9 oz/1 cup) whole-egg
  mayonnaise

3 tablespoons tomato sauce (ketchup)

2 teaspoons worcestershire sauce

½ teaspoon lemon juice

1 drop Tabasco sauce

1 kg (2 lb 4 oz) cooked medium prawns
  (shrimp)

lettuce leaves

lemon wedges

sliced bread

1   **For the cocktail sauce,** mix all the ingredients together in a bowl and season with salt and pepper.

2   **Peel the prawns,** leaving some with their tails intact to use as a garnish. Remove the tails from the rest. Gently pull out the dark vein from each prawn back, starting at the head end. Add the prawns without tails to the sauce and mix to coat.

3   **Arrange lettuce in serving** dishes or bowls. Spoon some prawns into each dish. Garnish with reserved prawns, drizzling with some dressing. Serve with lemon wedges and bread.

Note: Cocktail sauce can be made several hours ahead and stored in the refrigerator. Stir in 2 tablespoons thick (double/ heavy) cream for a creamier sauce.

CHARGRILLED BABY OCTOPUS

SERVES 4

1 kg (2 lb 4 oz) baby octopus

185 ml (6 fl oz/¾ cup) red wine

2 tablespoons balsamic vinegar

2 tablespoons soy sauce

2 tablespoons hoisin sauce

1 garlic clove, crushed

1 **Cut off the octopus** heads, below the eyes, with a sharp knife. Discard the heads and guts. Push the beaks out with your index finger, remove and discard. Wash the octopus thoroughly under running water and drain on paper towels. If the octopus are very large, cut the tentacles into quarters.

2 **Put the octopus** in a large bowl. Stir together the wine, vinegar, soy sauce, hoisin sauce and garlic in a bowl and pour over the octopus. Toss to coat, then cover and refrigerate for several hours, or overnight.

3 **Heat a chargrill** plate or barbecue hotplate until very hot and then lightly grease. Drain octopus, reserving the marinade. Cook in batches for 3–5 minutes, or until octopus flesh turns white. Brush the marinade over the octopus during cooking.

4 **Be careful** not to overcook or the octopus will be tough. Serve warm or cold. Delicious with a salad and lime wedges.

ASPARAGUS WITH SMOKED SALMON AND EGGS

SERVES 4

175 g (6 oz) butter

4 egg yolks

1 tablespoon lime juice

4 eggs, at room temperature

310 g (11 oz) asparagus spears

200 g (7 oz) smoked salmon

shaved parmesan cheese

1 To make the hollandaise sauce, melt the butter in a small saucepan and skim any froth from the surface. Remove from the heat. In a separate saucepan, mix the egg yolks with 2 tablespoons water. Place over very low heat and whisk for 30 seconds, or until pale and foamy, then continue whisking for 2–3 minutes, or until the whisk leaves a trail—do not overheat or the eggs will scramble. Remove from the heat. Add the cooled butter a little at a time, whisking well between each addition. Avoid using the milky whey at the bottom of the pan. Stir in the lime juice and season. If the sauce is still runny, return to the heat and whisk vigorously until thick, taking care not to scramble.

2 Half fill a saucepan with water and add the eggs. Bring to the boil and cook for 6–7 minutes, stirring occasionally to centre the yolks.

3 Drain and cool the eggs, then peel and quarter.

4 Bring a large saucepan of lightly salted water to the boil. Add the asparagus and cook for 3 minutes, or until just tender. Drain and pat dry. Divide the asparagus and smoked salmon among four serving plates. Arrange eggs over the top. Spoon on hollandaise and top with the parmesan cheese.

GREAT TASTES QUICK SHORT RECIPES

CIABATTA BREAKFAST TOASTS

SERVES 4

4 roma (plum) tomatoes, halved
2 large field mushrooms, halved
oil spray
8 slices bacon
160 g (6 oz/⅔ cup) cottage cheese
2 tablespoons chopped flat-leaf (Italian) parsley
1 tablespoons snipped chives
8 slices ciabatta bread, cut thickly at an angle and toasted
balsamic vinegar, to drizzle

1 **Preheat the grill** (broiler). Place the tomatoes, cut side up, and the mushrooms on a large baking tray. Lightly spray with the oil. Season well with black pepper. Pat the bacon dry with paper towels and place on the tray. Grill the tomatoes, mushrooms and bacon for 5–8 minutes, or until cooked. Turn the bacon slices once and remove them as they cook and become crisp.

2 **Combine the cottage** cheese, parsley and chives. Spread thickly over the toasted bread. Arrange the tomatoes, mushrooms and bacon over the top. Drizzle with a little balsamic vinegar.

Note: Ciabatta is an oval-shaped, dense, crusty Italian bread. It is available from delicatessens. If you can't find it, you can use sourdough or another type of bread.

FRESH SPRING ROLLS

MAKES 8

½ barbecued (grilled) chicken (see Note)

50 g (2 oz) dried mung bean vermicelli

8 x 17 cm (6½ inch) square dried rice paper wrappers

16 Thai basil leaves

1 large handful coriander (cilantro) leaves

1 carrot, cut into short thin strips and blanched

2 tablespoons plum sauce

1 **Remove the meat** from the chicken carcass, discard skin and finely shred the meat. Soak the vermicelli in hot water for 10 minutes and then drain. Dip a rice paper wrapper into warm water until it softens; place it on a clean work surface. Put one-eighth of the chicken in the centre of the wrapper and top with 2 basil leaves, a few coriander leaves and carrot strips and a small amount of vermicelli. Spoon a little plum sauce over the top.

2 **Press the filling** down to flatten it a little, then fold in the two sides and roll it up tightly like a parcel. Lay the rolls seam side down, on a serving plate and sprinkle with a little water. Cover with a damp tea towel (dish towel) and repeat the process with the remaining ingredients. Serve with your favourite dipping sauce or a little extra plum sauce.

Note: When buying the barbecued (grilled) chicken, ask for two breast quarters. Rice paper wrappers must be kept moist or they become brittle. If you leave the spring rolls for any length of time and they start to dry out, sprinkle cold water on them.

CHICKPEA FRITTERS

MAKES 6

2 tablespoons oil

4 spring onions (scallions), sliced

2 garlic cloves, chopped

600 g (1 lb 5 oz) tinned chickpeas, rinsed and drained

1 egg

chutney, to serve

small cos (romaine) lettuce leaves, to serve

crusty bread, to serve

1 Heat 2 teaspoons of the oil in a large non-stick frying pan over medium heat. Add the spring onion and garlic and cook, stirring, for 1–2 minutes, or until the spring onion softens.

2 Put the chickpeas and spring onion mixture in a food processor. Process until the mixture starts to hold together. Transfer to a bowl and mix in the egg. Using your hands, shape the mixture into six even fritters.

3 Heat the remaining oil in a large non-stick frying pan over medium heat. Add the chickpea fritters (cook in two batches if necessary) and cook for 2 minutes on each side, or until golden. Serve with chutney, lettuce and crusty bread.

MINI SWEET POTATO AND LEEK FRITTATAS

MAKES 12

1 kg (2 lb 4 oz) orange sweet potato

1 tablespoon olive oil

30 g (1 oz) butter

4 leeks, white part only, thinly sliced

2 garlic cloves, crushed

250 g (9 oz/1⅔ cup) crumbled feta cheese

8 eggs

125 ml (4 fl oz/½ cup) pouring cream

1 **Preheat the oven** to 180°C (350°F/Gas 4). Grease twelve 125 ml (4 fl oz/½ cup) muffin tin holes. Cut small rounds of baking paper and place into the base of each hole. Cut the sweet potato into small cubes and boil, steam or microwave until tender. Drain well and set aside.

2 **Heat the oil** and butter in a large frying pan, add leek and cook for about 10 minutes, stirring occasionally, or until very soft and lightly golden. Add the garlic and cook for 1 minute more. Cool, then stir in the feta and sweet potato. Divide the mixture evenly among the muffin holes.

3 **Whisk the eggs** and cream together and season with salt and freshly ground black pepper. Pour the egg mixture into each hole until three-quarters filled, then press the vegetables down gently. Bake for 25–30 minutes, or until golden and set. Leave in the tins for 5 minutes, then ease out with a knife and cool on a wire rack before serving.

GOAT'S CHEESE, LEEK AND TAPENADE PARCELS

SERVES 4

110 g (4 oz) butter

4 leeks, white part only, thinly sliced

8 sheets filo pastry

2 tablespoons tapenade

4 small rounds of goat's cheese or
   4 thick slices off a log of goat's cheese

4 small thyme sprigs

1 **Preheat the oven** to 180°C (350°F/Gas 4). Melt half the butter in a saucepan, add the leek and stir until it is coated in butter. Cook slowly over low heat until it is completely tender.

2 **Melt the rest** of the butter in a small saucepan on the stove. Place one of the sheets of filo on the work surface with the short end facing you. Brush the pastry with the melted butter. Lay another sheet right on top of it and cover it with a tea towel to stop the pastry drying out. Do the same with the other six sheets until you have four filo stacks.

3 **When the leek** is cooked, uncover the filo. Spread a quarter of the tapenade over the middle of each piece of pastry, leaving a wide border around the edges. Divide leeks among the filo, putting it on the tapenade. Top each pile of leek with the goat's cheese and then a thyme sprig. Now fold the bottom bit of pastry up and the two sides in, to enclose the filling, then fold the top end of the pastry down and roll the whole parcel over. Repeat with the remaining parcels.

4 **Brush the pastry** with the butter and bake the parcels for 20 minutes. Pastry should be browned and the filling melted.

MUSHROOMS WITH MARINATED FETA

SERVES 4

2 large oxheart tomatoes

20 fresh asparagus spears

300 g (10½ oz) marinated feta cheese

3 tablespoons extra virgin olive oil

zest of 1 lemon

2 garlic cloves, crushed

2 tablespoons lemon juice

4 large field mushrooms, brushed clean and stems removed

4 eggs

oregano, to garnish

1 Cut the tomatoes into thick slices. Trim the ends from the asparagus.

2 Drain the oil from the feta and place into a non-metallic bowl. Stir in the olive oil, lemon zest, garlic and lemon juice. Season with cracked black pepper.

3 Place the mushrooms and tomatoes in a shallow dish and pour the oil mixture over them. Toss gently to coat, and marinate for 15 minutes. Drain the mushrooms, reserving the marinade, and cook them, together with the tomatoes, on a lightly oiled barbecue grill plate until tender.

4 Add the asparagus towards the end of cooking, and lastly the eggs. Place mushrooms on a plate, top each one with some asparagus spears, a slice of tomato, an egg and some sliced feta. Drizzle with the oil marinade and garnish with oregano.

BAKED POTATOES WITH CHEESY BROAD BEANS

SERVES 4

4 large potatoes
300 g (10½ oz) broad (fava) beans
4 tablespoons cream
120 g (4 oz) blue cheese, crumbled
4 handfuls rocket (arugula), chopped

1   Heat the oven to 200°C (400°F/Gas 6). Wash the potatoes and, while they are still damp, rub them with a little coarse salt. Prick them several times and then put them in the oven, sitting directly on the oven shelf. This will help them get a good all-round heat. Bake for 1 hour, then squeeze gently—they should be soft. If they're still hard, give them another 15 minutes or so.

2   Cook the broad beans in boiling water for 3 minutes, then drain them well. Peel off the outer grey skins (optional).

3   When the potatoes are cooked, cut a cross in one side of each and squeeze the potatoes around the middle until they open up.

4   Put the cream in a small saucepan, add the broad beans, cook gently for a minute or two, then add the blue cheese and rocket. Stir everything together and when the rocket has wilted, spoon mixture into potatoes. Season with black pepper.

PORK SAN CHOY BAU

MAKES 25

1 tablespoon oil

400 g (14 oz) minced (ground) pork

230 g (8 oz) tinned water chestnuts,
    drained and finely chopped

125 g (4½ oz) tinned bamboo shoots,
    drained and finely chopped

6 spring onions (scallions), finely
    chopped

2 tablespoons dry sherry

1 tablespoon soy sauce

2 teaspoons sesame oil

2 teaspoons oyster sauce

tiny lettuce leaves, such as cos
    (romaine), iceberg or witlof (chicory/
    Belgian endive)

chopped mint, to serve

SAUCE

2 tablespoons plum sauce

1 tablepoon hoisin sauce

1 teaspoon soy sauce

1 Heat the oil in a frying pan or wok, add pork and cook, stirring, over high heat until brown all over. Break up lumps of pork with the back of a fork. Add the water chestnuts, bamboo shoots and spring onion. Toss well and cook for 1 minute.

2 Combine the sherry, soy sauce, sesame oil and oyster sauce. Add to the wok, toss well and cook for 2 minutes. Remove from the heat.

3 For dipping sauce, combine all the ingredients in a bowl with 2 tablespoons water.

4 To serve, put about 1 tablespoon of warm pork mixture on each lettuce leaf. Sprinkle with the chopped mint. Drizzle the sauce over the top.

Note: Pork can be prepared early in the day and refrigerated. Reheat to serve. The dipping sauce can be mixed a day ahead and refrigerated.

SCALLOP FRITTERS

250 g (9 oz) scallops

6 eggs

25 g (1 oz) parmesan cheese, grated

3 garlic cloves, crushed

125 g (4½ oz/1 cup) plain (all-purpose) flour

2 tablespoons chopped thyme

2 tablespoons chopped oregano

oil, for pan-frying

whole-egg mayonnaise, to serve (available in jars from supermarkets)

1 Clean and roughly chop the scallops. Lightly beat the eggs and combine with the parmesan, garlic, flour and herbs. Stir in the scallops.

2 Heat 2.5 cm (1 inch) oil in a deep frying pan to 180°C (350°F), or until a cube of bread dropped into the oil turns golden brown in 15 seconds. Cook fritters in batches, using 1 tablespoon of batter for each fritter, pouring it into the oil and cooking for 4–5 minutes, until golden brown. Drain on crumpled paper towels. Sprinkle lightly with salt. Serve with mayonnaise for dipping.

CHEESY BUBBLE AND SQUEAK CAKES WITH BACON

SERVES 4

4 large or 8 small floury potatoes

2 tablespoons milk

2 tablespoons butter

480 g (1 lb 1 oz) savoy cabbage, shredded

120 g (4 oz/1 cup) cheddar cheese, grated

1 tablespoon oil

8 bacon slices

1 Cut the potatoes into pieces and cook them in simmering water for 15 minutes, or until soft. Drain well, put them back in the pan with the milk and mash until they are smooth. Season with salt and pepper.

2 Melt the butter in a non-stick frying pan and cook the cabbage until it is soft. Add this to the potato along with the cheese. The mixture should be stiff enough to form the potato into cakes—it is up to you whether you make large ones or small ones.

3 Heat the oil in the same frying pan over medium heat and cook the bacon on both sides until it is crisp. Remove the bacon from the pan, keep warm. Add the potato cakes to the pan and fry them on both sides until they are well browned and slightly crisp. Shake the pan occasionally to move cakes around so they don't stick. Serve with the bacon.

MINI QUICHES LORRAINE

MAKES 12

2 sheets frozen ready-rolled shortcrust (pie) pastry, thawed

1 tomato, chopped

60 g (2 oz/½ cup) grated cheddar cheese

3 tablespoons chopped ham or bacon

1 spring onion (scallion), finely chopped

125 ml (4 fl oz/½ cup) milk

1 egg

1   Preheat the oven to 200°C (400°F/Gas 6). Cut the pastry into 12 rounds using an 8 cm (3¼ inch) cutter. Line 12 shallow patty pans or mini muffin tins with the pastry.

2   Combine the tomato, cheese, ham and spring onion and spoon the mixture into the pastry cases.

3   Whisk together the milk and egg. Pour enough into each pastry case to cover the filling.

4   Bake in the oven for 15–20 minutes, or until filling is set and golden. Transfer to a wire rack to cool. Store in the refrigerator in an airtight container for up to 2 days.

BARBECUED HALOUMI

MAKES 10

10 slices baguette

olive oil

1 garlic clove, crushed

250 g (9 oz) haloumi cheese, cut into
5 mm (¼ inch) slices

2 tablespoons chopped mint

1   Lightly brush the bread on both sides with some olive oil. Cook on a hot barbecue hotplate on both sides until brown.

2   Combine a little more oil with the crushed garlic and brush over the cheese. Cook on the barbecue hotplate for 1 minute, or until soft and golden underneath. Use a spatula to remove the cheese and place some on each piece of toast. Drizzle with a little more olive oil and sprinkle with mint and some freshly ground black pepper.

PITTA PIZZAS

4 large wholemeal (whole-wheat) pitta pocket breads

140 g (5 oz/½ cup) ready-made tomato salsa

½ red onion, thinly sliced

90 g (3 oz) mushrooms, thinly sliced

60 g (2 oz) good-quality ham, thinly sliced

90 g (3 oz/½ cup) black olives, pitted and chopped

1 tablespoons capers, rinsed, drained and chopped

80 g (3 oz/½ cup) feta

a few rosemary sprigs

100 g (3½ oz/⅔ cup) grated mozzarella cheese

1 **Preheat the oven** to 200°C (400°F/Gas 6). Place the pitta breads on a large baking tray or on two smaller trays. Spread each with the salsa. Scatter over the onion, mushrooms, ham, olives and capers.

2 **Crumble over the feta** and top with the rosemary sprigs and mozzarella. Bake for 20 minutes. Serve immediately.

Variations: Use tomato pasta sauce or salsa sauce on the base, then choose from the following toppings: ham, pineapple pieces, sliced capsicum (pepper), onion or olives.

For a meaty topping, try leftover savoury mince (ground meat) or spaghetti bolognaise and cheddar cheese. For a little spice, try salami, corn kernels, sliced green capsicum (pepper), onion, tomato and feta cheese.

A tasty vegetarian option is artichoke hearts, tomato and zucchini (courgette) slices, ricotta and feta cheese.

An easy seafood version uses tuna, sliced mushroom and capsicum and cheddar cheese (pepper).

CRUNCHY CHICKEN BITS

SERVES 4–6

oil, for greasing

1 kg (2 lb 4 oz) boneless, skinless
   chicken thighs or breasts

40 g (¼ cup) plain (all-purpose) flour

2 eggs

300 g (10½ oz) plain potato crisps,
   crushed

1 **Preheat the oven** to 180°C (350°F/Gas 4). Lightly grease two baking trays.

2 **Cut the chicken** into 2.5 cm (1 inch) pieces. Coat the chicken lightly in the flour, then dip in the combined mixture of the egg and 2 tablespoons water. Roll in the potato crisps, pressing on firmly.

3 **Lay out the** chicken in a single layer on the prepared trays and bake for about 15–20 minutes, or until cooked through and golden brown. Turn once during cooking.

Note: For an extra crunchy chicken bit, deep-fry in hot oil until cooked and golden brown.

BEAN ENCHILADAS

SERVES 4

1 tablespoon olive oil

1 onion, thinly sliced

3 garlic cloves, crushed

1 bird's eye chilli, finely chopped

2 teaspoons ground cumin

125 ml (4 fl oz/½ cup) vegetable stock

3 tomatoes, peeled, seeded and chopped

1 tablespoon tomato paste (concentrated purée)

2 x 425 g (15 oz) tins three-bean mix

2 tablespoons chopped coriander (cilantro) leaves

8 flour tortillas

1 small avocado, peeled and chopped

125 g (4½ oz/½ cup) sour cream

a few coriander (cilantro) sprigs

115 g (4 oz/2 cups) shredded lettuce

1   Heat oil in a deep frying pan over medium heat. Add the onion and cook for 3–4 minutes, or until just soft. Add garlic and chilli and cook for a further 30 seconds. Add the cumin, vegetable stock, tomato and tomato paste and cook for about 6 minutes, or until the mixture is quite thick and pulpy. Season with salt and freshly ground black pepper.

2   Preheat the oven to 170°C (325°F/Gas 3). Rinse and drain the beans. Add the beans to the sauce and cook for 5 minutes to heat through, then add the chopped coriander.

3   Meanwhile, wrap the tortillas in baking foil and warm in the oven for 3–4 minutes.

4   Place a tortilla on a plate and spread with a quarter of the bean mixture. Top with some avocado, sour cream, coriander sprigs and lettuce. Repeat with remaining tortillas. Roll up the enchiladas, tucking in the ends. Cut each one in half to serve.

LEEK, ZUCCHINI & CHEESE FRITTATA

SERVES 4

2 tablespoons olive oil

3 leeks, white part only, thinly sliced

2 zucchini (courgettes), cut into matchstick pieces

1 garlic clove, crushed

5 eggs, lightly beaten

4 tablespoons grated parmesan cheese

4 tablespoons diced gruyère or Swiss cheese

1 Heat 1 tablespoon of the olive oil in small ovenproof pan. Add leek and cook, stirring, over low heat until slightly softened. Cover and cook the leek for 10 minutes, stirring occasionally. Add the zucchini and garlic and cook for another 10 minutes. Transfer mixture to a bowl. Allow to cool, then season with freshly ground black pepper. Add the egg and cheeses and stir through.

2 Heat the remaining oil in the pan, add the egg mixture and smooth the surface. Cook over a low heat for 15 minutes, or until the frittata is almost set.

3 Put the pan under a preheated hot grill (broiler) for 3–5 minutes, or until the top is set and golden. Allow the frittata to stand for 5 minutes before cutting it into wedges. Serve with a fresh green salad.

CLASSIC OMELETTE

SERVES 4

12 eggs
40 g (1½ oz) butter

1 **Break the eggs** into a bowl. Add 8 tablespoon water, season with salt and freshly ground black pepper, and beat together well. Heat a quarter of the butter in a small frying pan or omelette pan over high heat. When the butter is foaming, reduce the heat to medium and add one-quarter of the egg mixture. Tilt the pan to cover the base with egg and leave for a few seconds. Using a spatula draw the sides of the omelette into the centre and let any extra liquid egg run to the edges.

2 **If you are adding** a filling to the omelette, sprinkle it over the egg. As soon as the egg is almost set, use a spatula to fold the omelette in half in the pan. It should still be soft inside. Slide it onto a warm serving plate and repeat to make 3 more omelettes.

Fillings: Sprinkle each omelette with a handful of roughly torn rocket and 50 g (2 oz) crumbled goat's cheese.

Sauté 250 g (9 oz) finely sliced button mushrooms with 50 g (2 oz) butter, add 4 tablespoons finely chopped basil and use some of the mixture for scattering over each omelette.

SPANISH OMELETTE WITH SMOKED SALMON

SERVES 4

1 tablespoon olive oil

400 g (14 oz) potatoes, cubed

1 onion, finely chopped

8 eggs

2 tablespoons dill, chopped

8 slices smoked salmon

4 tablespoons mascarpone cheese

4 handfuls salad leaves

1 Heat the oil in a non-stick frying pan and add the potato cubes. Fry gently, stirring them so they brown on all sides and cook through to the middle. This should take 10 minutes. Cut a cube open to see if they are cooked through completely.

2 When the potato is cooked, add the onion and cook it gently for a few minutes until it is translucent and soft. Switch on the grill (broiler).

3 When the onion is almost ready, break the eggs into a bowl and whisk them together with some salt and freshly ground pepper and the dill.

4 Tear the smoked salmon into pieces and add it to the frying pan. Add the mascarpone in blobs. Using a spatula, pull the mixture into the centre of the pan and level it off.

5 Pour the eggs over the top and cook for 5–10 minutes, or until the omelette is just set.

6 Put the frying pan under the grill for 1-2 minutes to lightly brown the top of the omelette. Slide the omelette out of the frying pan and cut it into eight wedges. Arrange a handful of salad leaves on each plate. Top with two wedges of omelette.

BAGELS WITH SMOKED SALMON AND CAPER SALSA

SERVES 4

4 plain or rye bagels

100 g (3½ oz) neufchatel cream cheese or other cream cheese

200 g (7 oz) sliced smoked salmon

2 spring onions (scallions), chopped

2 roma (plum) tomatoes, finely chopped

2 tablespoons baby capers, rinsed and squeezed dry

2 tablespoons finely chopped fresh dill

2 tablespoons lemon juice

1 tablespoon extra virgin olive oil

1 Cut the bagels in half and spread the base generously with cream cheese, then top with the salmon.

2 Combine spring onion, tomato, capers, dill, lemon juice and olive oil in a bowl. Pile mixture onto the salmon and serve.

TOFU FAJITAS

SERVES 4

4 tablespoons light soy sauce

2 garlic cloves, crushed

1 teaspoon ground black pepper

400 g (14 oz) smoked tofu, cut into 5 cm (2 inch) strips

200 g (7 oz) tinned tomatoes

1 small onion, roughly chopped

1 small red chilli, seeded and finely chopped

3 tablespoons chopped coriander (cilantro) leaves

1 large ripe avocado

2 teaspoons lemon juice

250 g (9 oz/1 cup) sour cream

2 tablespoons oil

1 red capsicum (pepper), seeded and membrane removed, sliced

1 yellow capsicum (pepper), seeded and membrane removed, sliced

8 spring onions (scallions), cut into 5 cm (2 inch) lengths

8 large (15 cm/6 inch) flour tortillas

1 **Place the soy** sauce, garlic and pepper in a shallow dish. Add tofu and toss together well. Cover and leave to marinate.

2 **Combine the tomatoes,** onion, chilli and coriander in a food processor until smooth. Season with salt and pepper. Transfer to a small saucepan, and bring to the boil. Reduce the heat and simmer for 10 minutes. Cool.

3 **Halve the avocado** and remove the stone. Scoop out the flesh and add the lemon juice and 2 tablespoons of the sour cream. Season and mash well with a fork.

4 **Heat 1 tablespoon** oil in a frying pan. Add the tofu and the remaining marinade and cook, stirring, over high heat for about 4 minutes. Remove from the pan. Heat the remaining oil in the pan.

5 **Add the capsicum** and spring onion, season and cook for 3–4 minutes.

6 **Dry-fry the tortillas** over high heat for 5 seconds on each side.

7 **To serve,** spread a tortilla with a little of the avocado mixture, the tomato salsa and sour cream. Top with some tofu and vegetables, fold in one end and roll. Repeat with remaining tortillas and fillings.

SAFFRON FISH CAKES WITH HERB CRÈME FRAÎCHE

SERVES 4

170 ml (5½ oz/⅔ cup) milk
2 pinches saffron threads
500 g (1 lb 2 oz) (about 4 medium fillets) white fish fillets
4 large potatoes, cut into chunks
2 garlic cloves, unpeeled
2 tablespoons plain (all-purpose) flour
2 teaspoons grated lemon zest
handful parsley, finely chopped
2 tablespoons cream
4 tablespoons crème fraîche
2 tablespoons mint, finely chopped
2 tablespoons parsley, finely chopped
1–2 tablespoons butter

1 Put the milk and saffron in a frying pan and heat until simmering. Add the fish, turn up the heat a little and cook until fish turns opaque and flaky—turn it over halfway through. Don't worry if it breaks up. Lift fish out of the milk into a bowl and break it up roughly with a fork. Set the milk aside.

2 Cook the potato and garlic clove in simmering water for about 12 minutes, or until the potato is tender. Drain the potato and put it back in the saucepan. Peel the garlic and add it to the potato, mash everything together and strain in the saffron milk. Keep mashing until the mixture is smooth, then stir in the fish, flour, 1 teaspoon of the lemon zest, the parsley and cream. Season well.

3 Shape the mixture into eight even-sized cakes. Put them in the fridge to chill while you make the herb crème fraîche by mixing together the crème fraîche, remaining lemon zest and herbs.

4 Heat the butter in a large non-stick frying pan and cook the fish cakes for 3 minutes on each side—they should have a brown crust. Serve with the crème fraîche.

SALT AND PEPPER SQUID

SERVES 4

125 g (4½ oz/1 cup) cornflour
(cornstarch)

1½ tablespoons salt

1 tablespoon ground white pepper

3 small red chillies, seeded and chopped

1 kg (2 lb 4 oz) cleaned squid tubes,
sliced into rings

2 egg whites, lightly beaten

oil, for deep-frying

lime wedges, for serving

1 **Combine the cornflour,** salt, pepper and chilli in a bowl.

2 **Dip the squid** rings into the egg white and then into the cornflour mixture. Shake off any excess cornflour.

3 **Fill a deep,** heavy-based saucepan one third full of oil and heat to 180°C (350°F), or until a cube of bread dropped into the oil browns in 15 seconds. Cook the squid in batches for 1–2 minutes, or until lightly golden all over. Drain on crumpled paper towels. Serve hot with steamed rice and lime wedges.

LEMON PEPPER TUNA BURGER

SERVES 4

2 x 185 g (6½ oz) tins lemon pepper tuna, drained

1 large onion, chopped

60 g (2 oz/⅔ cup) dry breadcrumbs

1 egg, lightly beaten

2 tablespoons chopped fresh lemon thyme and 1 tablespoon chopped flat-leaf (Italian) parsley (or a mixture of chopped fresh herbs or mixed dried herbs of your choice. If using dried, use half the amount specified here.)

2 teaspoons grated lemon zest

2 tablespoons oil

1 loaf Turkish bread

4 tablespoons whole-egg mayonnaise

150 g (5 oz) rocket (arugula)

4 slices cheddar cheese

2 tomatoes, sliced

1 cucumber, sliced

½ red onion, sliced

1 Mix tuna, onion, breadcrumbs, egg, thyme, parsley and lemon zest in a bowl. Form into four even-sized patties and flatten slightly. Heat a non-stick frying pan with the oil. Cook the patties over medium heat on both sides for 5 minutes, or until browned.

2 Cut the bread into four portions. Cut each portion in half horizontally and place under a grill (broiler) to lightly brown.

3 Spread both cut sides of the bread with mayonnaise. Top with some rocket and layer with a patty, a slice of cheese and slices of tomato, cucumber and onion. Place the other half of the Turkish bread on top, cut in half and serve.

THAI FRIED PRAWN BALLS

SERVES 4

600 g (1 lb 5 oz) raw prawns (shrimp),
  peeled and deveined

1 small handful coriander (cilantro)
  leaves

2 garlic cloves, chopped

2 egg whites

½ teaspoon salt

½ teaspoon ground white pepper

2–4 drops chilli oil, to taste

4 tablespoons peanut oil

sweet chilli sauce, to serve

1 Put the prawns, coriander leaves, garlic, egg whites, salt, pepper and chilli oil, to taste, in a small processor fitted with the metal blade. Whizz for 40 seconds, or until the mixture forms a paste.

2 Heat the peanut oil in a wok over medium–high heat. Using a metal spoon dipped in cold water, spoon heaped tablespoons of the prawn mixture into the oil. Fry, turning, for 3–4 minutes, or until golden brown. Drain on paper towels.

3 Serve the prawn balls immediately, accompanied by a cucumber salad and a small bowl of sweet chilli sauce.

FRESH SALMON PATTIES WITH MANGO SALSA

SERVES 6

1 garlic clove, peeled

500 g (1 lb 2 oz) fresh salmon, skin removed, roughly chopped (or use tinned, drained)

1 red onion, diced

50 g (2 oz/½ cup) dry breadcrumbs

1 egg

50 g (2 oz/1 cup) chopped coriander (cilantro)

1 mango, diced

3 tablespoons lime juice

1 Place the garlic, salmon and half the onion in a food processor. Process until coarsely minced. Add breadcrumbs, egg and half the coriander, and season. Combine well and divide into six equal portions. Shape into patties, place on a plate, cover and refrigerate for 30 minutes

2 To make the salsa, place the mango, 2 tablespoons lime juice and the remaining onion and coriander in a bowl, and mix together well.

3 Heat a lightly greased non-stick frying pan, add remaining lime juice and cook patties for 4–5 minutes each side. They should be moist and slightly pink inside. Distribute patties among six serving plates and spoon salsa on top. For a more substantial meal, serve patties with salad and bread.

MAINS

CHICKEN SKEWERS WITH SPICY CHILLI SAUCE

SERVES 4

SAUCE

2 lemon grass stems, white part only, chopped

8 coriander (cilantro) roots including 10 cm (4 inch) stems, chopped

7.5 cm (3 inch) piece galangal or ginger, chopped

1 large red Asian shallot, chopped

2 garlic cloves, chopped

1 large green chilli, seeded and chopped

3 large tomatoes

1 tablespoon oil

3 tablespoons fish sauce

3 tablespoons soft brown sugar

2 teaspoons tamarind concentrate (available from Asian supermarkets)

2 tablespoons chopped coriander (cilantro) leaves

750 g (1 lb 10 oz) boneless, skinless chicken breast, cubed

canola oil spray or olive oil spray

1   To make the sauce, put the lemon grass, coriander roots and stems, galangal, shallot, garlic and chilli in a small processor fitted with the metal blade. Whizz in 3–4 second bursts for 30 seconds, or until finely chopped.

2   Score a cross in the base of each tomato. Place tomatoes in a heatproof bowl and cover with boiling water. Leave for 20 seconds, then transfer to cold water and peel the skin away from the cross. Roughly chop the flesh.

3   Heat the oil in a large heavy-based saucepan. Add the lemon grass paste, stir, then add two-thirds of the chopped tomato. Cook, stirring, for 5 minutes. Set aside to cool slightly, then transfer to the processor and whizz for 15 seconds, or until smooth. Add the remaining tomato and whizz in short bursts for 15 seconds, or until the mixture is finely chopped but still has texture.

4   Return the mixture to the saucepan and add the fish sauce, sugar and tamarind concentrate. Simmer, stirring frequently, for 10 minutes. Stir in the coriander leaves.

5   Thread the chicken onto metal skewers and brush with oil. Preheat the barbecue or chargrill pan to high and cook the chicken, turning frequently, for 5–7 minutes, or until just cooked through. Serve with the sauce.

BATTERED FISH AND CHUNKY WEDGES

SERVES 4

3 all-purpose potatoes

oil, for deep-frying

150 g (5 oz/1 cup) self-raising flour

1 egg, beaten

185 ml (6 fl oz/¾ cup) beer (fizzy or flat)

4 white fish fillets

plain (all-purpose) flour, for dusting

125 g (4½ oz/½ cup) ready-made
    tartare sauce

1   **Wash the potatoes,** but do not peel them. Cut into thick wedges, then dry with paper towels. Fill a large heavy-based saucepan two-thirds full with oil and heat. Gently lower the potato wedges into medium–hot oil. Cook for 4 minutes, or until tender and lightly browned. Carefully remove the wedges from the oil with a slotted spoon and drain on paper towels.

2   **Sift the self-raising** flour with some freshly ground black pepper into a large bowl and make a well in the centre. Add the egg and beer. Using a wooden spoon, stir until just combined and smooth. Dust the fish fillets in the plain flour, shaking off the excess. Add the fish fillets one at a time to the batter and toss until well coated. Remove from the batter, draining off the excess.

3   **Working with one piece** of fish at a time, gently lower it into the medium–hot oil. Cook for 2 minutes, or until golden and crisp and cooked through. Carefully remove from the oil with a slotted spoon. Drain on paper towels, and keep warm while you cook the remainder. Return the potato wedges to the medium–hot oil. Cook for another 2 minutes, or until golden brown and crisp. Remove from the oil with a slotted spoon and drain on paper towels. Serve the wedges immediately with the fish and tartare sauce. If desired, serve with wedges of lemon and garnish with fresh dill.

Variation: You can serve the wedges with sour cream and sweet chilli sauce instead of tartare sauce.

SALMON FILLETS WITH LEMON HOLLANDAISE SAUCE

SERVES 4

LEMON HOLLANDAISE SAUCE

175 g (6 oz) butter

4 egg yolks

2 tablespoons lemon juice

2 tablespoons olive oil

4 salmon fillets with skin on

1 **Melt the butter** in a small saucepan over low heat. Skim any froth from the surface and discard. Leave to cool. Whisk the yolks and 2 tablespoons water in a separate small saucepan for 30 seconds, or until pale and foamy. Place the saucepan over very low heat and whisk the egg mixture for 2–3 minutes, or until it is frothy and the whisk leaves a trail behind it as you whisk. Don't let the saucepan get too hot or you will scramble the eggs. Remove from the heat.

2 **Add cooled butter** to the eggs, a little at a time, whisking well after each addition. Avoid using the milky whey from the base of the saucepan. Stir in the lemon juice and season with salt and cracked black pepper.

3 **Heat the oil** in a large non-stick frying pan over high heat and cook salmon fillet, skin side down, for 2 minutes. Turn it over and cook for 2 minutes, or until cooked to your liking. Serve with the sauce and salad or vegetables of your choice.

SALMON KEDGEREE

SERVES 4

1 litre (35 fl oz/4 cups) fish stock

400 g (14 oz) salmon fillet

3 tablespoons butter

2 tablespoons oil

1 onion, chopped

2 teaspoons madras curry paste

200 g (7 oz/1 cup) long-grain rice

2 hard-boiled eggs, cut into wedges

3 tablespoons chopped parsley

3 tablespoons cream

lemon wedges, to serve

1   Put the stock in a frying pan and bring to the boil. Put the salmon in the stock, cover, then reduce the heat to a simmer. Cook for 3 minutes, or until it becomes firm when pressed and turns opaque. Lift out the salmon and flake it into large pieces by gently pulling it apart with your hands.

2   Melt half of the butter in a frying pan with the oil, add the onion and cook over a low heat until the onion softens and turns translucent. Stir in the curry paste, then add the rice and mix well until the rice is coated. Add the fish stock, mix well, then bring the mixture to the boil.

3   Simmer the rice, covered, over a very low heat for 8 minutes, then add the salmon and cook, covered, for another 5 minutes, until all the liquid is absorbed. If the rice is too dry and not cooked, add a splash of boiling water and keep cooking for a further 1–2 minutes.

4   Stir in the rest of the butter, the eggs, parsley and cream (you can leave out the cream if you prefer—the result won't be so rich). Serve the kedgeree with the lemon wedges to squeeze over.

ROAST CHICKEN WITH WILD RICE

SERVES 8

1 teaspoon salt

200 g (7 oz/1 cup) wild rice

200 g (7 oz/1 cup) jasmine rice

1 Chinese barbecued roast chicken
(see Note)

3 tablespoons chopped mint

3 tablespoons chopped coriander
(cilantro)

1 large Lebanese (short) cucumber

6 spring onions (scallions)

80 g (3 oz/½ cup) roasted peanuts,
roughly chopped

4 tablespoons mirin

2 tablespoons Chinese rice wine

1 tablespoon soy sauce

1 tablespoon lime juice

2 tablespoons sweet chilli sauce,
plus extra, to serve

1 Bring a large saucepan of water to the boil and add the salt and the wild rice. Cook for 30 minutes, add the jasmine rice and cook for a further 10 minutes, or until tender. Drain the rice, refresh under cold water and drain again.

2 Shred the chicken (the skin as well) into bite-sized pieces and place in a large bowl and add mint and coriander. Cut the cucumber through the centre (do not peel) and slice thinly on the diagonal. Slice the spring onions on the diagonal. Add the cucumber, spring onion, rice and peanuts to the bowl with the chicken.

3 Combine the mirin, rice wine, soy, lime juice and sweet chilli sauce in a small bowl, pour over the salad and toss to combine. Pile the salad onto serving platters and serve with extra chilli sauce.

Note: It is important to use a Chinese barbecued chicken, available from Chinese barbecue shops. The flavours of five-spice and soy used to cook it will add to the flavour of the dish.

PRAWN PULAO

SERVES 4

200 g (7 oz/1 cup) basmati rice

300 g (10½ oz) small prawns (shrimp)

3 tablespoons oil

1 onion, finely chopped

1 cinnamon stick

6 cardamom pods

5 cloves

1 lemon grass stalk, finely chopped

4 garlic cloves, crushed

5 cm (2 inch) piece of ginger, grated

¼ teaspoon ground turmeric

1 **Wash the rice** under cold running water and drain. Peel and devein the prawns, then wash and pat dry with paper towels.

2 **Heat the oil** in a frying pan over a low heat and fry the onion, spices and lemon grass. Stir in the garlic, ginger and turmeric. Add the prawns and stir until pink. Toss in the rice and fry for 2 minutes. Pour in 500 ml (17 fl oz/2 cups) of boiling water and add a pinch of salt. Bring to the boil. Reduce the heat and simmer for 15 minutes. Remove from the heat, cover and leave for 10 minutes. Fluff up rice before serving.

SPAGHETTI CARBONARA

SERVES 4

1 tablespoon olive oil

300 g (10½ oz) pancetta, cut into small dice

170 ml (6 fl oz/⅔ cup) thick (double/heavy) cream

6 egg yolks

400 g (14 oz) spaghetti

60 g (2 oz/⅔ cup) grated parmesan cheese

1 Heat the oil in a saucepan and cook the pancetta, stirring frequently, until it is light brown and crisp. Tip the pancetta into a sieve to strain off any excess oil.

2 Mix the cream and egg yolks together in a bowl, and when the pancetta has cooled, add it to the egg mixture.

3 Cook the spaghetti in a large saucepan of boiling salted water until al dente, stirring once or twice to make sure the pieces are not stuck together. Drain the spaghetti and reserve a small cup of the cooking water.

4 Put the spaghetti back in the saucepan and put it over a low heat. Add the egg mixture and half the parmesan, then take the pan off the heat, otherwise the egg will scramble. Season with salt and pepper and mix together. If the sauce is too thick and the pasta is stuck together, add a little of the reserved cooking water. The spaghetti should look as if it has a fine coating of egg and cream all over it.

5 Serve the spaghetti in warm bowls with more parmesan sprinkled over the top.

FRESH TOMATO AND BASIL SAUCE WITH PASTA

SERVES 4

400 g (14 oz) spaghetti

5 tablespoons extra virgin olive oil

5 garlic cloves, thinly sliced

6 vine-ripened tomatoes, seeded
and chopped

1 large handful basil leaves, torn

1   **Cook the pasta** in a large saucepan of boiling salted water until al dente, stirring once or twice to make sure the pieces are stuck together. Drain the pasta. If the pasta will be sitting around for a little while before being added to the sauce, return it to the pan and toss through a little olive oil to prevent it from sticking together.

2   **While the pasta** is cooking, heat 4 tablespoons of the oil in a frying pan and cook the garlic over low heat for 1 minute. As soon as the garlic begins to change colour, remove the pan from the heat and add the remaining oil.

3   **Add the cooked pasta** to the pan with the tomato and basil. Season generously with salt and ground black pepper. Toss well and serve drizzled with a little extra virgin olive oil.

SALMON WITH MISO AND SOY NOODLES

SERVES 6

300 g (10½ oz) soba noodles

1 tablespoon soy bean oil

3 teaspoons white miso paste (from Japanese supermarkets)

100 ml (3½ fl oz) honey

1½ tablespoons sesame oil, plus 1 teaspoon, extra

6 salmon fillets, boned and skin removed

1 teaspoon chopped garlic

1 tablespoon grated ginger

1 carrot, cut into very thin strips

6 small spring onions (scallions), thinly sliced

70 g (2½ oz/1 cup) bean sprouts

4 tablespoons rice vinegar

3 tablespoons light soy sauce

1 tablespoon sesame seeds, toasted

mustard cress, to garnish

1 Preheat the oven to 180°C (350°F/Gas 4). Fill a large saucepan three-quarters full with water and bring to the boil. Add the soba noodles and return to the boil. Cook for 1 minute, then add 250 ml (9 fl oz/1 cup) cold water. Boil for 1–2 minutes, then add another 250 ml (9 fl oz/1 cup) water. Boil for 2 minutes, or until tender, then drain and toss with ½ teaspoon of the soy bean oil.

2 Combine the miso, honey, sesame oil and 1 tablespoon water to form a paste. Brush over the salmon, then sear on a hot chargrill for 30 seconds on each side. Brush the salmon with the remaining paste and place on a baking tray. Bake for 6 minutes, then cover and rest in a warm place.

3 Heat remaining soy oil in a wok. Add the garlic, ginger, carrot, spring onion and bean sprouts, and stir-fry 1 minute; the vegetables should not brown, but remain crisp and bright. Add the noodles, rice vinegar, soy sauce and extra sesame oil and stir-fry briefly to heat through.

4 Divide the noodles among six serving plates and top with a portion of salmon and sprinkle with the sesame seeds. Garnish with the mustard cress and serve.

FARFALLE WITH PRAWNS AND HORSERADISH CREAM

SERVES 4

400 g (14 oz) farfalle or other decorative pasta shape

1 tablespoon olive oil

2 French shallots, sliced

800 g (1 lb 12 oz/about 32) tiger prawns or other large prawns (shrimp), peeled and deveined

2 tablespoons lemon juice

125 ml (4 fl oz/½ cup) cream

2 teaspoons grated lemon zest

2 tablespoons horseradish cream

2 tablespoons chervil

1   Cook the farfalle in a large saucepan of boiling salted water until al dente, stirring once or twice to make sure the pieces do not stick together.

2   Heat the oil in a frying pan and add the shallot. Cook for a minute, then add the prawns. Cook over high heat for 2–3 minutes, or until the prawns have turned bright pink and are cooked through. Add lemon juice and toss well. Turn off the heat and leave everything in the pan.

3   Put the cream in a glass bowl and whisk it until it just starts to thicken. Don't make it too thick because when you add the lemon zest and lemony prawns the acid will thicken it further. Fold the lemon zest, horseradish cream and chervil into the cream.

4   Drain the farfalle and tip it into a large bowl. Add prawns and any lemon juice to the bowl, then add the cream mixture. Fold everything together and season with salt and pepper.

RICE NOODLES WITH BEEF AND BLACK BEANS

SERVES 4

300 g (10½ oz) rump steak

1 garlic clove, crushed

3 tablespoons oyster sauce

2 teaspoons sugar

2 tablespoons soy sauce

100 ml (3½ fl oz) black bean sauce

2 teaspoons cornflour (cornstarch)

¾ teaspoon sesame oil

1.2 kg (2 lb 11 oz) fresh or 600 g
   (1 lb 5 oz) dried flat rice noodles

1½ tablespoons oil

2 red capsicums (peppers), sliced

1 green capsicum (pepper), sliced

1 handful coriander (cilantro) leaves

1 Cut the steak across the grain into thin slices and put it in a bowl with the garlic, oyster sauce, sugar, soy sauce, black bean sauce, cornflour and sesame oil. Mix everything together, making sure the slices are all well coated.

2 Soak dried rice noodles, if using, in boiling water for about 10 minutes, or until they are opaque and soft. If your noodles are particularly dry, they may need a little longer. Then drain.

3 Heat the oil in a wok or frying pan and, when it is hot, add the capsicums. Stir-fry the capsicums for 1-2 minutes until they are starting to soften, then add the meat mixture and cook for a minute. Add the noodles and toss everything together well. Keep cooking until the meat is cooked through and everything is hot, then toss in the coriander leaves and stir once before turning off the heat. Serve straight away.

SALT AND PEPPER CHICKEN WITH ASIAN GREENS

SERVES 4

250 g (9 oz/1¼ cups) jasmine rice

4 tablespoons plain (all-purpose) flour

¾ teaspoon five-spice powder

1½ teaspoons sea salt

1 teaspoon ground white pepper

750 g (1 lb 10 oz) boneless, skinless chicken breasts, cut into thin strips (1 x 5 cm/½ x 2 inch)

150 ml (5 fl oz) peanut oil

1.25 kg (2 lb 12 oz) mixed Asian greens (bok choy/pak choy, choy sum or gai lam)

125 ml (4 fl oz/½ cup) oyster sauce

1   **Bring a large saucepan** of water to the boil. Add the rice and cook for 12 minutes, stirring occasionally. Drain well.

2   **Meanwhile, combine the flour,** five-spice powder, salt and pepper in a large bowl. Toss the chicken strips in the flour until well coated. Heat 3 tablespoons of the oil in a large frying pan over medium–high heat. Add the chicken in three batches and cook, turning, for about 3 minutes, or until browned. Drain on crumpled paper towels and keep warm.

3   **Heat the remaining oil** and cook the mixed Asian greens over medium–high heat for 1–2 minutes. Add the oyster sauce and toss through. Serve on a bed of jasmine rice topped with the chicken strips.

SPICY SAUSAGES WITH HARISSA AND COUSCOUS

SERVES 4

2 tablespoons butter

280 g (10 oz/1½ cups) instant couscous

2 teaspoons harissa

3 tablespoons olive oil

2 tablespoons lemon juice

1½ tablespoons grated lemon zest

2 tablespoons parsley, chopped

150 g (5½ oz) chargrilled red capsicum
   (pepper), sliced

4 tablespoons raisins

12 merguez sausages

thick plain yoghurt, to serve

1 Put the butter in a saucepan with 500 ml (17 fl oz/2 cups) water and bring to the boil. Sprinkle in the couscous, mix it into the water, then take it off the stove. Put a lid on the pan and leave it to sit for 5 minutes. Turn on the grill (broiler). Stir the harissa, olive oil, lemon juice and zest together until well mixed. Add the parsley, red capsicum and raisins and leave everything to marinate briefly.

2 Grill the sausages for 8 minutes, turning them so they brown on all sides.

3 Meanwhile, take the lid off the couscous and stir it for 1-2 minutes to separate the grains. Stir in the harissa mixture.

4 Serve the couscous with the sausages sliced over it and topped with a large dollop of yoghurt.

LAMB CUTLETS WITH SPICY YOGHURT SAUCE

SERVES 4

SAUCE

1 large green chilli, seeded and chopped

1 large handful mint

1 red Asian shallot, chopped

2.5 cm (1 inch) piece ginger, chopped

2 teaspoons fish sauce

2 teaspoons lime juice

1 teaspoon shaved palm sugar (jaggery)
  or soft brown sugar

250 g (9 oz/1 cup) Greek-style yoghurt

oil, for cooking

12–16 French-trimmed lamb cutlets
  (see Notes)

1 **To make the sauce,** put the chilli, mint, shallot, ginger, fish sauce, lime juice and sugar in a small processor fitted with the metal blade. Whizz for 30 seconds, or until the mixture forms a rough paste. Transfer to a small bowl and stir in the yoghurt. Cover and refrigerate until needed.

2 **Brush a chargrill** pan with oil, heat over high heat and add the cutlets in a single layer. Cook for 2 minutes on each side, or until the cutlets are browned on the outside but still feel springy when pressed. Season well with salt and freshly ground black pepper.

3 **Arrange the cutlets** on a serving plate and serve with the sauce.

Notes: French-trimmed lamb cutlets have the bones trimmed of fat and sinew. Ask your butcher to prepare the cutlets for you.

Couscous or potato mash are ideal accompaniments to this dish. Store the sauce, covered, in the refrigerator for up to 2 days.

CHILLI LINGUINE WITH CHERMOULA CHICKEN

SERVES 4

600 g (1 lb 5 oz) skinless, boneless
   chicken breasts

500 g (1 lb 2 oz) chilli linguine

CHERMOULA

100 g (3½ oz/2 cups) coriander
   (cilantro), leaves, chopped

60 g (2 oz/2 cups) flat-leaf (Italian)
   parsley leaves, chopped

4 garlic cloves, crushed

2 teaspoons ground cumin

2 teaspoons ground paprika

125 ml (½ cup) lemon juice

2 teaspoons lemon zest

100 ml (3½ fl oz) olive oil

1 Heat a large non-stick frying pan over medium heat. Add the chicken breasts and cook until tender. Remove from the pan and leave or 5 minutes before cutting into thin slices.

2 Cook the pasta in a large saucepan of boiling salted water until al dente, stirring once or twice to make sure the pieces are not stuck together, then drain.

3 Meanwhile, combine the chermoula ingredients in a glass bowl and add the sliced chicken. Leave to stand until the pasta has finished cooking. Serve the pasta topped with the chermoula chicken.

CHICKEN WITH PEACH, CAPSICUM AND BEAN SALSA

SERVES 4

oil spray

4 skinless, boneless chicken breasts

3 fresh peaches

150 g (5½ oz) baby green beans, trimmed

3 tablespoons white wine vinegar

1 tablespoon caster (superfine) sugar

2 teaspoon grated ginger

1 garlic clove, crushed

½ teaspoon ground cumin

3 tablespoons chopped coriander (cilantro) leaves

3 tablespoons chopped mint

1 red capsicum (pepper), diced

1 small red onion, finely diced

1 small red chilli, finely chopped

1 **Lightly spray a chargrill** pan or barbecue hotplate with oil and cook the chicken breasts for 5 minutes on each side, or until tender and cooked through.

2 **Meanwhile, to peel** the peaches, briefly plunge them into a bowl of boiling water. Refresh under cold water, then slip the skins from the peaches. Remove stones; dice the flesh.

3 **Blanch the beans** in a saucepan of boiling water for 2 minutes, then drain and refresh.

4 **Combine vinegar, sugar,** ginger, garlic, cumin, coriander and mint in a small bowl.

5 **Put the capsicum,** onion, chilli, peaches and beans in a large bowl. Gently stir through the vinegar herb mixture and serve at once with the chicken.

LINGUINE WITH ROASTED CHERRY TOMATOES

SERVES 4

400 g (14 oz) linguine

500 g (1 lb 2 oz) red cherry tomatoes

500 g (1 lb 2 oz) yellow cherry tomatoes

2 tablespoons olive oil

2 garlic cloves, crushed

4 spring onions (scallions), sliced

1 bunch chives, finely chopped

100 g (3½ oz/about 20) black olives

extra virgin olive oil, for drizzling

1 Cook the linguine in a large saucepan of boiling salted water until al dente, stirring once or twice to make sure the pieces are not stuck together.

2 Cut all the cherry tomatoes in half. Heat the oil in a saucepan, add the garlic and spring onion and let them sizzle briefly. Tip in the cherry tomatoes and cook them over high heat until they just start to collapse and give off their juices. Add the chives and olives, season with salt and pepper and toss everything together well.

3 Drain the linguine and put it in a large serving bowl or individual bowls. Pour the cherry tomato mixture on top and grind some black pepper over the top. Drizzle with a little bit more olive oil if you like.

ORECCHIETTE WITH SMOKED MOZZARELLA

SERVES 4

400 g (14 oz) orecchiette

2 tablespoons olive oil

150 g (5½ oz) sliced pancetta, cut into short thin strips

200 g (7 oz) button mushrooms, sliced

2 leeks, white part only, sliced

250 ml (9 fl oz/1 cup) cream (see Note)

200 g (7 oz) smoked mozzarella (mozzarella affumicata), cut into 1 cm (½ inch) cubes (see Note)

8 basil leaves, roughly torn

1 **Cook the orecchiette** in a large saucepan of rapidly boiling salted water until al dente, stirring once or twice to make sure the pieces are not stuck together.

2 **Meanwhile, heat the oil** in a large frying pan and sauté the pancetta, mushrooms and leek over medium–high heat for 5 minutes. Stir in the cream and season with pepper—the pancetta should provide enough salty flavour. Simmer over low heat for 5 minutes, or until the pasta is ready. Drain the pasta and stir into the frying pan. Add mozzarella and basil and toss lightly.

Note: If you are watching your weight, you can use half chicken stock and half cream instead of all cream. Smoked provolone can be used instead of the mozzarella, if preferred.

RACK OF LAMB WITH HERB CRUST

SERVES 4

2 x 6–rib racks of lamb, French-trimmed

1 tablespoon oil

80 g (3 oz/1 cup) fresh breadcrumbs

3 garlic cloves

3 tablespoons finely chopped flat-leaf (Italian) parsley

2 teapoons thyme leaves

½ teaspoon finely grated lemon zest

60 g (2¼ oz) butter, softened

250 ml (9 fl oz/1 cup) beef stock

1 garlic clove, extra, finely chopped

1 thyme sprig

1   Preheat the oven to 250°C (500°F/Gas 9). Score the fat on the lamb racks in a diamond pattern. Rub with a little oil and season.

2   Heat the oil in a frying pan over high heat, add the lamb racks and brown for 4–5 minutes. Remove and set aside. Do not wash the pan as you will need it later.

3   In a large bowl, mix the breadcrumbs, garlic, parsley, thyme leaves and lemon zest. Season, then mix in the butter to form a paste.

4   Firmly press a layer of breadcrumb mixture over the fat on the lamb racks, leaving the bones and base clean. Bake in a roasting tin for 12 minutes for medium–rare. Rest the lamb on a plate while you make the jus.

5   To make the jus, add the beef stock, extra garlic and thyme sprig to the roasting tin juices, scraping the pan. Return this liquid to the original frying pan and simmer over high heat for 5–8 minutes, or until the sauce has reduced. Strain and serve with the lamb.

CHICKEN BREAST WITH GOAT'S CHEESE

SERVES 4

4 large skinless, boneless chicken breasts

100 g (3½ oz) semi-dried (sun-blushed) tomatoes

100 g (3½ oz) goat's cheese, sliced

200 g (7 oz) asparagus spears, trimmed, halved and blanched

50 g (2 oz) butter

375 ml (13 fl oz/1½ cups) chicken stock

2 zucchini (courgettes), cut into strips 5 cm (2 inches) long

250 ml (9 fl oz/1 cup) cream

8 spring onions (scallions), thinly sliced

1 **Pound each chicken** breast between two sheets of plastic wrap with a mallet or rolling pin until 1 cm (½ in) thick. Divide the tomato, goat's cheese and 150 g (5½ oz) of the asparagus pieces among the breasts. Roll up tightly lengthways, securing along the seam with toothpicks.

2 **Heat the butter** in a large frying pan over medium heat. Add the chicken, then brown on all sides. Pour in the stock, then reduce the heat to low. Cook, covered, for 10 minutes, or until the chicken is cooked through. Remove the chicken and keep warm.

3 **Meanwhile, bring a saucepan** of lightly salted water to the boil. Add the zucchini and remaining asparagus and cook for 2 minutes, or until just tender. Remove from the pan. Whisk the cream into the frying pan. Add the spring onion and simmer over medium–low heat for 4 minutes, or until reduced and thickened. To serve, cut each chicken roll in half on the diagonal and place on serving plates. Spoon on the sauce and serve with the greens.

SALMON WITH BEAN PURÉE

SERVES 4

4 x 175 g (6 oz) salmon fillets

2 teaspoons canola oil

1 garlic clove, crushed

2 tablespoons white wine vinegar

1 teaspoon finely grated lime zest

2 tablespoons chopped dill

600 g (1 lb 5 oz) tin cannellini (white) beans, rinsed and drained

1 bay leaf

250 ml (9 fl oz/1 cup) chicken stock

500 g (1 lb 2 oz/1 bunch) baby English spinach leaves, roughly chopped

1   **Place the salmon** in a non-metallic dish. Combine the oil, garlic, vinegar, lime zest and dill, pour over the fish, then cover and leave to stand for 10 minutes.

2   **Place the beans,** bay leaf and stock in a saucepan, and simmer for 10 minutes. Remove the bay leaf. Place in a food processor and purée. Season well with salt and freshly ground black pepper.

3   **Drain the salmon,** reserving the marinade. Cook in a non-stick frying pan over a high heat for 3–5 minutes on each side, or until crisp and golden. Remove, add the marinade to the pan and boil.

4   **Steam the spinach** until wilted. Serve the salmon fillets on the purée and spinach and drizzle over the marinade. Serve with chunky slices of brown bread.

SEAFOOD PASTA

SERVES 4

12 black mussels, scrubbed clean and beards removed

125 ml (4 fl oz/½ cup) white wine

1 teaspoon olive oil

1 large onion, chopped

3 garlic cloves, finely chopped

2 x 400 g (14 oz) tins chopped tomatoes

2 tablespoons tomato paste (concentrated purée)

1 teaspoon dried oregano

500 g (1 lb 2 oz) bucatini or spaghetti (see Note)

8 raw prawns (shrimp), peeled and deveined, tails intact

300 g (10½ oz) fresh or frozen seafood marinara mixture

1 large handful basil, shredded

1 **Discard any opened mussels.** Place mussels in a large saucepan with the wine and 125 ml (4 fl oz/½ cup) water. Cook, covered, for 3 minutes, or until mussels have opened. Discard any unopened ones. Remove the mussels from the pan and reserve the liquid.

2 **Heat the oil** in a large saucepan, add the onion and garlic and cook for 2–3 minutes, or until softened. Add the tomatoes, tomato paste and oregano leaves. Stir in the reserved mussel cooking juice. Bring to the boil, then simmer for 20 minutes, or until reduced and thickened a little.

3 **Meanwhile, cook the pasta** in a large saucepan of boiling salted water until just tender, stirring once or twice to make sure the pieces are not stuck together. Drain.

4 **Add the prawns** and marinara mixture to the sauce. Cook over a low heat for 3 minutes, or until the seafood is cooked. Toss the sauce, mussels and basil through the pasta. Serve immediately.

Note: You can use any thick pasta shape, such as penne, or wide, long pasta such as pappardelle.

STUFFED PRAWN OMELETTES

MAKES 8

500 g (1 lb 2 oz) raw prawns (shrimp)

1½ tablespoons oil

4 eggs, lightly beaten

2 tablespoons fish sauce

8 spring onions (scallions), chopped

6 coriander (cilantro) roots, chopped

2 garlic cloves, chopped

2 small red chillies, seeded and chopped

2 teaspoons lime juice

2 teaspoons grated palm sugar (jaggery) or soft brown sugar

3 tablespoons chopped coriander (cilantro) leaves, plus sprigs, to garnish

sweet chilli sauce, to serve

1 Peel the prawns, gently pull out and discard the dark vein from each prawn back, starting from the head end, then chop the prawn meat.

2 Heat a wok over high heat, add 2 teaspoons of the oil and swirl to coat. Combine the egg with half of the fish sauce. Add 2 tablespoons of the mixture to the wok and swirl to a 15 cm (6 inch) round. Cook for 1 minute, then gently lift out. Repeat with the remaining egg mixture to make eight omelettes.

3 Heat the remaining oil in the wok. Add the prawns, spring onion, coriander root, garlic and chilli. Stir-fry for 3–4 minutes, or until the prawns are cooked. Stir in lime juice, palm sugar, coriander leaves and the remaining fish sauce.

4 Divide prawn mixture among the omelettes and fold each into a small firm parcel. Cut a slit in the top and garnish with the chilli and coriander sprigs. Serve with sweet chilli sauce

SESAME-COATED TUNA WITH CORIANDER SALSA

SERVES 4

4 tuna steaks

115 g (4 oz/¾ cup) sesame seeds

100 g (3½ oz) baby rocket (arugula)
leaves

chilli jam, to serve (optional)

CORIANDER SALSA

2 tomatoes, seeded and diced

1 large garlic clove, crushed

2 tablespoons finely chopped coriander
(cilantro) leaves

2 tablespoons olive oil, plus extra for
shallow-frying

1 tablespoon lime juice

1 Cut each tuna steak into 3 pieces. Place the sesame seeds on a sheet of baking paper. Roll the tuna in the sesame seeds to coat. Refrigerate for 15 minutes.

2 To make the salsa, place the tomato, garlic, coriander, oil and lime juice in a bowl, and mix together well. Cover and refrigerate until ready to use.

3 Fill a heavy-based frying pan to 1.5 cm (⅝ inch) with the extra oil and place over high heat. Add the tuna in two batches and cook for 2 minutes each side (it should be pink in the centre). Remove and drain on paper towels. To serve, divide the rocket among four serving plates and arrange the tuna over the top. Spoon the salsa on the side and serve immediately. Top with a teaspoon of chilli jam, if desired, and season well.

SURF 'N' TURF

SERVES 4

LEMON MUSTARD SAUCE

30 g (1 oz) butter

1 spring onion (scallion), finely chopped

1 garlic clove, crushed

1 tablespoon plain (all-purpose) flour

250 ml (9 fl oz/1 cup) milk

2 tablespoons pouring cream

1 tablespoon lemon juice

2 teaspoons dijon mustard

1 large or 2 small raw lobster tails

2 tablespoons oil

4 beef eye fillets (200 g/7 oz each)

175 g (6 oz) fresh or frozen crabmeat

flat-leaf (Italian) parsley, to garnish

1 To make the sauce, melt the butter in a saucepan, add the spring onion and garlic and stir over medium heat for 1 minute, or until the onion has softened. Stir in the flour and cook for 1 minute, or until pale and foaming. Remove from the heat and gradually stir in the milk. Return to the heat and stir constantly until the sauce boils and thickens. Reduce the heat and simmer for 2 minutes. Remove from the heat and stir in the cream, lemon juice and mustard. Keep warm.

2 Starting at the end where the head was, cut down each side of the lobster shell on the underside with kitchen scissors. Pull back the flap and remove the meat from the shell. Heat half the oil in a frying pan, add the lobster meat and cook over medium heat for 3 minutes each side (longer if using a large tail), or until just cooked through. Remove from the pan and keep warm. Reserve the oil in the pan.

3 Heat remaining oil in a separate frying pan, add steaks and cook over high heat for 2 minutes each side to seal, turning once. For rare steaks, cook each side 1 more minute. For medium and well-done steaks, reduce heat to medium and continue cooking for 2–3 minutes each side for medium or 4–6 minutes each side for well done. Remove from the pan and keep warm.

4 Add the crab to the reserved lobster pan and stir until heated through. To serve, place the steaks on plates. Top with crab followed by slices of lobster. Pour the sauce over the top and garnish with parsley.

STEAK WITH MAÎTRE D'HOTEL BUTTER

SERVES 4

90 g (3¼ oz) unsalted butter, softened

2 teaspoons finely chopped parsley

lemon juice

4 steaks, about 1.5 cm (⅝ inch) thick

1 tablespoon olive oil

1 Beat the butter to a cream in a bowl, using a wooden spoon, then beat in a pinch of salt, a pinch of pepper and the parsley. Next add about 2 teaspoons of lemon juice, a few drops at a time. Let the butter harden in the fridge a little, then form it into a log shape by rolling it up in greaseproof paper. Put it into the fridge until you need it.

2 Season the steaks with salt and pepper on both sides. Heat the oil in a large frying pan and, when it is very hot, add the steaks. Cook them for 2 minutes on each side for rare, 3 minutes on each side for medium, and 4 minutes on each side for well done. The timings may vary depending on the thickness of your steaks—if they are thin, give them a slightly shorter time and if they are thick, cook them for longer.

3 Cut the butter into slices and put a couple of slices on top of each steak. The heat of the steak will melt the butter. Serve with potatoes and vegetables or salad.

CHICKEN AND VEGETABLE PASTA

SERVES 4

3 (500 g/1 lb 2 oz) small, single boneless, skinless chicken breasts

1½ tablespoons oil

1 large leek, white part only, halved lengthways, thinly sliced

2 garlic cloves, crushed

150 g (5½ oz) green beans, diagonally sliced into 2.5 cm (1 inch) pieces

2 celery stalks, trimmedand sliced

250 ml (9 fl oz/1 cup) chicken stock

300 g (10½ oz) rice pasta spirals

1   Heat a large non-stick frying pan over medium heat. Brush the chicken with 2 teaspoons of the oil. Cook the chicken breast fillets for 4 minutes on each side, or until cooked through. Transfer to a plate, cover loosely with foil and set aside.

2   Heat the remaining oil in the same pan over medium heat. Add the leek and cook, stirring often, for 6–7 minutes, or until almost soft.

3   Add the garlic, beans and celery. Cook for 2–3 minutes, or until the vegetables are tender. Increase the heat to high and pour in the stock. Simmer for 2–3 minutes, or until the liquid reduces slightly.

4   Meanwhile, cook the pasta in a large saucepan of boiling salted water until al dente, stirring once or twice to make sure the pieces are not stuck together. Drain and return to the pan.

5   Slice the chicken across the grain. Add to the pasta along with the vegetables and sauce. Season to taste with salt. Toss until well combined. Serve immediately.

Note: This recipe has been made using rice pasta spirals, a gluten-free product, but you can also use regular pasta spirals if you prefer.

VEGETABLE AND VEAL PASTA

SERVES 4

1½ tablespoons oil

1 leek, white part only, thinly sliced

100 g (3½ oz) swede (rutabaga), peeled and chopped

100 g (3½ oz) potatoes, peeled and chopped

2 garlic cloves, crushed

400 g (14 oz) cabbage, core removed, shredded

500 g (1 lb 2 oz) minced (ground) lean veal

2 teaspoons cornflour (cornstarch)

375 ml (12 fl oz/1½ cups) beef/veal stock

375 g (13 oz) rice pasta

1 Heat 1 tablespoon of the oil in a large non-stick frying pan over medium heat. Add the leek, swede, potato and garlic. Cook, stirring often, for 5–6 minutes, or until the vegetables are almost tender. Add the cabbage and 2 tablespoons water. Cover and cook for a further 7–8 minutes, or until the cabbage is tender. Remove the vegetables from the pan.

2 Heat the remaining oil in the pan over high heat. Add the veal and cook, stirring, for 3–4 minutes, or until well browned. In a bowl, combine the cornflour with a little of the stock, then add the remaining stock and a little salt. Add the stock mixture to the veal with the vegetables and stir until boiling. Reduce the heat and simmer for 2–3 minutes, or until the sauce thickens.

3 Meanwhile, cook the pasta in a large saucepan of boiling salted water until al dente, stirring once or twice to make sure the pieces are not stuck together. Drain and return to the pan.

4 Divide the pasta among four serving plates. Top with the meat and vegetable mixture and serve immediately.

Note: This recipe has been made using rice pasta spirals, a gluten-free product, but you can also use regular pasta spirals if you prefer.

PORK CHOPS IN MARSALA

SERVES 4

4 pork loin chops

2 tablespoons olive oil

125 ml (4 fl oz/½ cup) Marsala (or sweet sherry or port)

2 teaspoons grated orange zest

3 tablespoons orange juice

3 tablespoons chopped flat-leaf (Italian) parsley

1 Pat dry the chops and season well. Heat the olive oil in a heavy-based frying pan over medium heat and cook the chops on both sides for 5 minutes each side, or until brown and cooked.

2 Add the Marsala, orange zest and juice and cook for 4–5 minutes, or until the sauce has reduced and thickened. Add the parsley and serve with vegetables.

SALTIMBOCCA

SERVES 4

8 small veal escalopes

8 slices prosciutto

8 sage leaves

2 tablespoons olive oil

60 g (2¼ oz) butter

185 ml (6 fl oz/¾ cup) dry Marsala or dry
white wine

1 Place the veal between two sheets of baking paper and pound with a meat mallet or rolling pin until they are 5 mm (¼ inch) thick. Make sure you pound them evenly. Peel off the paper and season lightly. Cut the prosciutto slices to the same size as the veal. Cover each piece of veal with a slice of prosciutto and place a sage leaf in the centre. Secure the sage leaf with a cocktail stick.

2 Heat the olive oil and half the butter in a large frying pan. Add the veal in batches and fry, prosciutto side up, over medium heat for 3–4 minutes, or until the veal is just cooked through. Briefly flip the saltimbocca over and fry the prosciutto side. Transfer each batch to a warm plate as it is done.

3 Pour off the oil from the pan and add the Marsala or wine. Bring to the boil and cook over high heat until reduced by half, scraping up the bits from the bottom of the pan. Add the remaining butter and, when it has melted, season the sauce. Remove the cocktail sticks and spoon the sauce over the veal.

PAPRIKA GARLIC CHICKEN

SERVES 6

1 kg (2 lb 4 oz) boneless, skinlesss chicken thighs

1 tablespoon paprika

2 tablespoons olive oil

8 garlic cloves, unpeeled

3 tablespoons brandy

125 ml (4 fl oz/½ cup) chicken stock

1 bay leaf

2 tablespoons chopped flat-leaf (Italian) parsley

1   Trim any excess fat from the chicken and cut the thighs into thirds. Combine the paprika with some salt and pepper in a bowl, add the chicken and toss to coat.

2   Heat half the olive oil in a large frying pan over medium heat and cook the garlic for 1–2 minutes, until brown. Remove from the pan. Increase the heat to high and cook the chicken in batches for 5 minutes each batch, or until brown. Return all the chicken to the pan, add brandy and boil for 30 seconds, then add the stock and bay leaf. Reduce the heat, cover and simmer over low heat for 10 minutes.

3   Meanwhile, peel the garlic and put it in a mortar or small bowl. Add the parsley and pound with the pestle or crush with a fork to form a paste. Stir into the chicken, then cover and cook for 10 minutes, or until tender. Serve hot.

GREEK-STYLE LAMB

SERVES 4

400 g (14 oz) lean lamb fillets

1 teaspoon olive oil

1 large red onion, sliced

3 zucchini (courgettes), thinly sliced

200 g (7 oz) cherry tomatoes, halved

3 garlic cloves, crushed

60 g (2¼ oz/½ cup) pitted black olives in brine, drained and cut in half

2 tablespoons lemon juice

2 tablespoons finely chopped oregano

100 g (3½ oz) feta cheese, crumbled

4 tablespoons pine nuts, lightly toasted

1   **Trim the lamb,** then cut across the grain into thin strips. Heat a large frying pan until hot and brush with a little olive oil. Add the lamb in small batches and cook each batch over high heat for 1–2 minutes, or until browned. Remove all the lamb from the pan.

2   **Heat the oil** in the pan, then add the onion and zucchini. Cook, stirring, over high heat for 2 minutes, or until just tender. Add the cherry tomatoes and garlic. Cook for 1–2 minutes, or until the tomatoes have just softened. Return the meat to the pan and stir over high heat until heated through.

3   **Remove the pan** from the heat. Add the olives, lemon juice and oregano and toss until well combined. Sprinkle with crumbled feta cheese and pine nuts before serving. Serve with bread and a mixed green salad.

FISH ROLLS

SERVES 4

1 large ripe tomato

1 tablespoon capers, rinsed and squeezed dry, chopped

40 g (1½ oz) stuffed green olives, chopped

3 tablespoons chopped lemon thyme

30 g (1 oz) romano cheese, finely grated

2 teaspoons finely grated lemon zest

¼ teaspoon black pepper

8 thin firm skinless white fish fillets, such as john dory, bream, perch, snapper

250 ml (9 fl oz/1 cup) dry white wine

2 tablespoons lemon juice

3 tablespoons lemon thyme

2 bay leaves

1 **Preheat the oven** to 160°C (315°F/Gas 2–3). Score a cross in the base of the tomato. Place in a heatproof bowl and cover with boiling water. Leave for 30 seconds, then transfer to cold water and peel away the skin. Cut in half and scoop out the seeds. Roughly chop the flesh and mix with the capers, olives, thyme, cheese, lemon zest and black pepper, in a small bowl.

2 **Place the fillets,** skinned side up, on a flat surface. Spread the tomato mixture evenly onto each fillet, then roll tightly and secure with a toothpick or skewer. Place in a single layer in a shallow casserole dish.

3 **Pour the combined** wine, lemon juice, thyme and bay leaves over the fish, cover and bake for 20 minutes, or until the fish is cooked and flakes easily when tested with a fork.

FISH FILLETS WITH FENNEL AND RED CAPSICUM SALSA

SERVES 4

750 g (1 lb 10 oz) small new potatoes

1 teaspoon fennel seeds

125 ml (4 fl oz/½ cup) olive oil

2 tablespoons, rinsed and squeezed dry, baby capers

1 small red capsicum (pepper), seeded and finely diced

250 g (9 oz) mixed salad leaves, washed and picked over

2 tablespoons balsamic vinegar

4 white fish fillets (blue eye cod or John Dory), about 200 g/7 oz each

1 **Cook the potatoes** in a saucepan of boiling water for 15–20 minutes, or until tender. Drain and keep warm.

2 **Meanwhile, to make** the salsa, dry-fry the fennel seeds in a frying pan over medium heat for 1 minute, or until fragrant. Remove the seeds and heat 1 tablespoon oil in the same pan over medium heat. When the oil is hot but not smoking, flash-fry the capers for 1–2 minutes, or until crisp. Remove from the pan. Heat 1 tablespoon oil and cook the capsicum, stirring, for 4–5 minutes, or until cooked through. Remove and combine with the fennel seeds and fried capers.

3 **Place the salad leaves** in a serving bowl. To make the dressing, combine the balsamic vinegar and 3 tablespoons of the olive oil in a bowl. Add 1 tablespoon to the salsa, then toss the rest through the salad leaves.

4 **Wipe the frying pan,** then heat the remaining oil over medium–high heat. Season the fish well. When the oil is hot, but not smoking, cook the fish for 2–3 minutes each side, or until cooked through. Serve immediately with the salsa, potatoes and salad.

SPICE-CRUSTED SALMON AND NOODLE SALAD

SERVES 4

½ teaspoon wasabi paste

4 tablespoons Japanese soy sauce

100 (3½ fl oz) mirin

1 teaspoon sugar

250 g (9 oz) dried somen noodles

1 teaspoon sesame oil

1 teaspoon sansho powder (see Note)

1 tablespoon vegetable oil

¼ teaspoon salt

3 salmon fillets (about 200 g each),
skin removed

4 spring onions (scallions), finely sliced
on the diagonal

1 large handful coriander (cilantro)
leaves

1 Lebanese (short) cucumber, halved
lengthways, thinly sliced

1 **Combine the wasabi** with a little of the Japanese soy sauce to form a smooth paste. Stir in the mirin, sugar and remaining soy sauce.

2 **Cook the noodles** in a large saucepan of boiling salted water for 2 minutes, or until tender. Drain and rinse in cold water. Transfer to a large bowl and toss with the sesame oil.

3 **Combine sansho powder**, oil and salt and brush on both sides of the salmon. Heat a large frying pan over medium heat.

4 **Add the salmon** and cook each side for 2–3 minutes, or until cooked to your liking. Remove from the pan and flake into large pieces with a fork.

5 **Add the salmon,** spring onion, coriander, cucumber and half the dressing to the noodles, then toss together. Place on a serving dish and drizzle with the remaining dressing.

Note: Sansho powder has peppery lemon flavour with a touch of heat to it.

STEAMED LEMON GRASS AND GINGER CHICKEN

SERVES 4

200 g (7 oz) fresh thin rice noodles

4 boneless, skinless chicken breasts, trimmed

2 lemon grass stems

5 cm (2 inch) piece ginger, julienned

1 lime, thinly sliced

500 ml (17 fl oz/2 cups) chicken stock

350 g (12 oz/1 bunch) choy sum, cut into 10 cm (4 inch) lengths

800 g (1 lb 12 oz) Chinese broccoli (gai lam), cut into 10 cm (4 inch) lengths

3 tablespoons kecap manis

3 tablespoons soy sauce

1 teaspoon sesame oil

toasted sesame seeds, to garnish

1 Put the rice noodles in a large heatproof bowl, cover with boiling water and soak for 5 minutes, or until softened. Separate gently and drain. Cut each chicken breast horizontally through the middle so that you are left with eight thin flat chicken fillets.

2 Cut lemon grass into lengths that are about 5 cm (2 inch) longer than the chicken fillets, then cut in half lengthways. Discard tough outer leaves. Place one piece of lemon grass onto one piece of fillet, top with some ginger and lime slices, then top with another fillet.

3 Pour the stock into a wok and bring to a simmer. Put two chicken fillets in a paper-lined bamboo steamer and place the steamer over the wok. Steam over the simmering stock for 12–15 minutes, or until chicken is tender. Remove chicken from steamer, cover and keep warm. Repeat with other fillets.

4 Steam the greens in the same way for 3 minutes, or until tender. Bring the stock in the wok to the boil. Place the kecap manis, soy sauce and sesame oil in a bowl and whisk together well.

5 Divide the noodles among four plates and ladle the boiling stock over them. Top with a pile of Asian greens, then add the chicken and drizzle each serve with the sauce. Sprinkle with sesame seeds and serve.

Note: Kecap manis is an Indonesian sweet sauce similar to a soy sauce.

LAMB FILLET WITH PEA SAUCE

SERVES 4

2 tablespoons oil

800 g (1 lb 12 oz) lamb fillets

1 garlic clove, peeled and slivered

PEA SAUCE

155 g (5½ oz/1 cup) frozen peas

3 tablespoons parsley, chopped

3 spring onions (scallions), chopped

3 tablespoons pear juice

¼ teaspoon citric acid

3 tablespoons chicken stock

1 **Preheat the oven** to 180°C (350°F/Gas 4). Heat the oil in a roasting tin. Add the lamb fillets and garlic to the roasting tin. Bake for 8–10 minutes for medium or 12–15 minutes for well done.

2 **While the lamb** is cooking, prepare the pea sauce. Bring a small saucepan of water to the boil, add the peas, parsley and spring onion and cook for 2 minutes, or until the peas are bright green and tender. Drain, reserving 4 tablespoons of the cooking liquid. Purée the peas, reserved liquid, pear juice, citric acid and stock in a food processor or blender. Return the purée to the saucepan and heat over low heat until the sauce is heated through.

3 **Remove the lamb** from the oven. Slice and arrange on serving plates. Spoon the pea sauce to the side. If desired, serve potatoes cooked by the method of your choice.

CRISPY FISH AND LENTILS

SERVES 4

4 tablespoons plain (all-purpose) flour

4 (600 g/1 lb 5 oz) boneless white fish fillets

2 tablespoons oil

4 spring onions (scallions), diagonally sliced

2 garlic cloves, crushed

2 x 400 g (14 oz) tins brown lentils, rinsed and drained

250 g (9 oz) green beans, trimmed

1 **Combine the flour** and a little salt on a plate. Coat the fish fillets in seasoned flour, shaking off excess. Heat 1 tablespoon of the oil in a large non-stick frying pan over medium–high heat. Add the fish and cook for 3–4 minutes on each side, or until cooked through and lightly browned—depending on the size of your frying pan you may need to cook fish in batches.

2 **Meanwhile, heat the** remaining oil in a large saucepan. Cook the spring onion and garlic for 2 minutes, or until softened. Add the lentils. Toss for a few minutes, or until the lentils are heated through.

3 **Steam or microwave** the beans for a few minutes, or until just tender.

4 **Serve the fish** with warm lentils and the green beans.

KIDS' QUICK PASTA WITH TOMATO SAUCE

SERVES 4

1 tablespoon extra virgin olive oil

1 garlic clove, crushed

400 g (14 oz) tin diced roma (plum) tomatoes

250 g (9 oz/2¾ cups) penne or farfalle (bow tie pasta)

1 tablespoon shaved parmesan cheese

1 Heat the olive oil in a frying pan over medium heat. Cook the garlic, stirring constantly, for 30 seconds. Add the tomatoes and stir through. Reduce the heat to low and cook for a further 8–10 minutes, stirring occasionally, or until reduced.

2 Meanwhile, cook the pasta in a large saucepan of salted boiling water until just tender, stirring once or twice to make sure the pieces are not stuck together. Drain and return to the saucepan.

3 Add cooked tomatoes to the pasta and stir through.

4 Spoon the pasta into a bowl and sprinkle with parmesan cheese.

Variation: Stir through the tomato sauce a spoonful of mashed, drained tinned tuna and just cooked (not mushy) vegetables such as diced zucchini (courgettes), diced carrot, diced butternut pumpkin (squash), finely chopped baby spinach and finely chopped flat-leaf (Italian) parsley.

OPEN LASAGNE WITH ROCKET AND WALNUT PESTO

SERVES 4

PESTO

100 g (3½ oz/1 cup) walnuts

2 garlic cloves

2 large handfuls baby rocket (arugula)

1 large handful basil

1 large handful flat-leaf (Italian) parsley

100 ml (3½ fl oz) extra virgin olive oil

4 tablespoons walnut oil

50 g (2 oz/½ cup) grated pecorino cheese

100 g (3½ oz/1 cup) grated parmesan cheese

375 g (13 oz) fresh lasagne sheets

1 tablespoon olive oil

4 large handfuls baby spinach leaves

1 garlic clove, sliced

2 tablespoons lemon juice

200 g (7 oz) marinated goat's feta cheese, crumbled

2 tablespoons grated parmesan cheese

1 **To make the pesto,** preheat the oven to 180°C (350°F/ Gas 4). Rinse the walnuts in cold water, then shake dry. Spread the walnuts on a baking tray and bake for 5–8 minutes, or until lightly golden. Watch carefully as they will burn easily.

2 **Transfer the walnuts** to a small processor fitted with the metal blade. Add the garlic, rocket, basil and parsley and whizz in 3-second bursts for 1 minute, or until the mixture resembles coarse breadcrumbs. With the motor running, add the oils in a thin stream, then add the pecorino and parmesan and whizz for 40 seconds. Cover with plastic wrap and set aside.

3 **Cut lasagne sheets** into sixteen 7.5 cm (3 inch) squares. Cook a few squares at a time in a large saucepan of boiling salted water for 4 minutes, or until al dente. Lay them on a clean tea towel (dish towel) and cover to keep warm while the remaining squares are cooked.

4 **Heat the olive oil** in a large frying pan over medium heat, add the spinach and garlic and sauté until just wilted. Add the lemon juice and stir to combine. Cover and keep warm.

5 **Spoon 1 tablespoon** of the pesto onto four warmed plates and spread out with the back of the spoon to the size of one of the pasta squares. Cover with a pasta square, then divide one-third of the spinach over the pasta. Sprinkle with one-third of the goat's feta, cover with another pasta square and spread with the pesto. Repeat the layers, finishing with a layer of pesto. Sprinkle with the grated parmesan and serve immediately.

Note: Pesto is delicious spooned over steamed vegetables to accompany grilled (broiled) fish or meat. Store pesto, covered with a thin layer of olive oil, in an airtight container, in the refrigerator for up to 3 days.

LAMB KOFTAS IN PITTA BREAD

SERVES 4

500 g (1 lb 2 oz) lean lamb

1 onion, roughly chopped

1 large handful flat-leaf (Italian) parsley, roughly chopped

1 large handful mint, chopped

2 teaspoons grated lemon zest

1 teaspoon ground cumin

¼ teaspoon chilli powder

250 g (9 oz/1 cup) yoghurt

2 teaspoon lemon juice

oil spray

4 wholemeal (whole-wheat) pitta breads

taboulleh (a half-quantity of recipe on page 98), or use a small tub of shop-bought taboulleh

1   Roughly chop the lamb. Put the lamb and onion in a food processor and process until smooth. Add the parsley, mint, lemon zest and spices and process until well combined. Divide the mixture into 24 balls and place on a tray. Cover and refrigerate for at least 30 minutes to allow the flavours to develop.

2   To make the yoghurt dressing, combine yoghurt and lemon juice in a bowl. Cover and refrigerate.

3   Heat a large, non-stick frying pan. Spray with the oil. Cook lamb balls in two batches, spraying with the oil before each batch, until browned all over and cooked through.

4   Preheat the oven to 180°C (350°F/Gas 4). Cut the pitta pocket breads in half, wrap in foil and place in the oven for 10 minutes.

5   To serve, divide the tabbouleh between the pitta bread halves, add 3 kofta balls to each and top with the yoghurt dressing.

CAJUN CHICKEN WITH FRESH TOMATO AND CORN

SERVES 4

2 corn cobs

2 vine-ripened tomatoes, diced

1 Lebanese (short) cucumber, diced

2 tablespoons roughly chopped coriander (cilantro) leaves

4 boneless, skinless chicken breast (about 200 g/7 oz each)

3 tablespoons Cajun seasoning

2 tablespoons lime juice

lime wedges, to serve

1 **Cook the corn cobs** in a saucepan of boiling water for 5 minutes, or until tender. Remove the kernels using a sharp knife and place in a bowl with the tomato, cucumber and coriander. Season and mix well.

2 **Heat a chargrill** pan or barbecue plate to medium heat and brush lightly with oil. Pound each chicken breast between two sheets of plastic wrap with a mallet or rolling pin until 2 cm (¼ in) thick. Lightly coat the chicken with the Cajun seasoning and shake off any excess. Cook for 5 minutes on each side, or until just cooked through.

3 **Just before serving,** stir the lime juice into the salsa. Place a chicken breast on each plate and spoon the salsa on the side. Serve with the lime wedges, a green salad and crusty bread.

JOHN DORY WITH PRAWNS AND CREAMY DILL SAUCE

SERVES 4

12 raw large prawns (shrimp)

625 ml (21½ fl oz/2½ cups) fish stock

30 g (1 oz) butter

1 garlic clove, finely chopped

2 tablespoons plain (all-purpose) flour

2 tablespoons pouring cream

oil, for pan-frying

4 john dory fillets (200 g/7 oz each)

1 tablespoon snipped chives

1 tablespoon chopped dill

chives or dill sprigs, to garnish

1   Peel the prawns, leaving the tails intact. Gently pull out the dark vein from each prawn back, starting from the head end. Heat stock in a saucepan and bring to the boil. Reduce the heat and simmer for 10 minutes, or until the liquid has reduced. You will need 375 ml (13 fl oz/1½ cups) fish stock.

2   Melt the butter in a small saucepan and add the garlic. Stir in the flour and cook for 1 minute, or until pale and foaming. Remove from the heat and gradually stir in the stock. Return to the heat and stir constantly until the sauce boils and thickens. Reduce heat and simmer for 1 minute. Remove from heat and stir in the cream. Season to taste. Keep warm.

3   Heat a little oil in a frying pan and cook the fish fillets over medium heat for 2 minutes each side, or until the fish flakes easily when tested with a fork. Transfer to serving plates. Add the prawns to the same pan (add more oil to the pan if necessary) and cook for 2–3 minutes. Stir the chives and dill into the sauce, arrange the prawns on top of the fish and spoon the sauce over the top. Garnish with chives or dill.

TUNA STEAKS ON CORIANDER NOODLES

SERVES 4

3 tablespoons lime juice

2 tablespoons fish sauce

2 tablespoons sweet chilli sauce

2 teaspoons grated palm sugar (jaggery) or soft brown sugar

1 teaspoon sesame oil

1 garlic clove, finely chopped

1 tablespoon virgin olive oil

4 tuna steaks (150 g/5½ oz each), at room temperature

200 g (7 oz) dried thin wheat noodles

6 spring onions (scallions), thinly sliced

2 large handfuls chopped coriander (cilantro) leaves

lime wedges, to garnish

1 **To make the dressing,** place the lime juice, fish sauce, chilli sauce, sugar, sesame oil and garlic in a small bowl and mix together.

2 **Heat the olive oil** in a chargrill pan. Add the tuna steaks and cook over high heat for 2 minutes each side, or until cooked to your liking. Transfer the steaks to a warm plate, cover and keep warm.

3 **Place the noodles** in a large saucepan of lightly salted, rapidly boiling water and return to the boil. Cook for about 4 minutes, or until noodles are tender. Drain well. Add half the dressing and half the spring onion and coriander to the noodles and gently toss together.

4 **Either cut the tuna** into even cubes or slice it.

5 **Place the noodles** on serving plates and top with the tuna. Mix remaining dressing with the spring onion and coriander and drizzle over the tuna. Garnish with lime wedges.

Note: If you prefer, you can serve the tuna steaks whole rather than cutting them into cubes. If serving whole, they would look better served with the noodles on the side.

SALADS

CAESAR SALAD

SERVES 4–6

DRESSING

3 eggs

3 garlic cloves, crushed

2–3 anchovy fillets

1 teaspoon worcestershire sauce

2 tablespoons lime juice

1 teaspoon dijon mustard

185 ml (6 fl oz/¾ cup) olive oil

3 slices white bread

1 tablespoon butter

1 tablespoon oil, extra

3 slices bacon

1 large or 4 baby cos (romaine) lettuces

75 g (2½ oz/¾ cup) shaved parmesan cheese

1 **To make the** dressing, process the eggs, garlic, anchovies, worcestershire sauce, lime juice and mustard in a food processor until smooth. With the motor running, add the oil in a thin, continuous stream to produce a creamy dressing. Season to taste with salt and freshly ground black pepper.

2 **Cut the crusts** off the bread, then cut the bread into 1.5 cm (⅝ inch) cubes. Heat the butter and extra olive oil in a frying pan over medium heat, add the bread and cook for 5–8 minutes, or until crisp, then remove from the pan. Cook the bacon in the same pan for 3 minutes, or until it is crispy, then break into bite-sized pieces.

3 **Toss the lettuce leaves** with the dressing, then stir in the croutons and bacon, and top with parmesan cheese.

MODERN SALAD NIÇOISE

SERVES 4

DRESSING

3 tablespoons lemon juice

1 garlic clove, crushed

135 ml (4½ fl oz) olive oil

400 g (14 oz) waxy potatoes, such as kipfler (fingerling)

3 eggs

120 g (4 oz) green beans, trimmed

1 green capsicum (pepper), seeded and sliced

120 g (4½ oz/⅔ cup) black olives

300 g (10½ oz) firm, ripe tomatoes, cut into wedges

100 g (3½ oz) cucumber, cut into chunks

3 spring onions (scallions), cut into 2 cm (¾ inch) pieces

600 g (1 lb 5 oz) fresh tuna steaks

1   Place the lemon juice, garlic and 125 ml (4 fl oz/½ cup) olive oil in a jar with a screw-top lid. Season and shake the jar well to combine.

2   Boil the potatoes in a saucepan of salted water, for 10–12 minutes, or until tender. Add the eggs for the final 8 minutes of cooking. Drain, cool the eggs under cold water, then peel and quarter. Cool the potatoes, then cut into chunks. Bring a saucepan of salted water to the boil, add green beans and blanch for 3 minutes. Drain and refresh under cold water. Drain well, then slice in half on the diagonal.

3   Place the potato and beans in a large bowl, and add the capsicum, olives, tomato, cucumber and spring onion. Strain the garlic from the dressing, then shake again so it is combined. Pour half over the salad, toss and transfer to a serving dish.

4   Heat a frying pan over very high heat. Add remaining olive oil and allow to heat. Season the tuna steaks well on both sides and cook for 2 minutes on each side, or until rare. Allow tuna to cool for 5 minutes; slice thinly. Arrange on top of the salad with the eggs. Drizzle with remaining dressing.

GREEK SALAD

SERVES 4

4 tomatoes, cut into wedges

1 telegraph (long) cucumber, peeled, halved, seeded and cut into small cubes

2 green capsicums (peppers), seeded, halved lengthways and cut into strips

1 red onion, thinly sliced

16 kalamata olives

250 g (9 oz) firm feta cheese, cut into cubes

3 tablespoons flat-leaf (Italian) parsley

12 whole mint leaves

DRESSING

125 ml (4 fl oz/½ cup) olive oil

2 tablespoons lemon juice

1 garlic clove, crushed

1 **Place the tomato wedges,** cucumber, capsicum strips, onion, kalamata olives, feta and half of the parsley and mint leaves in a large serving bowl, and toss together gently.

2 **To make the** dressing, place the oil, lemon juice and garlic in a screw-top jar, season and shake until well combined. Pour the dressing over the salad and toss. Garnish with the remaining parsley and mint.

TUSCAN BREAD SALAD

SERVES 6

200 g (7 oz) ciabatta bread

8 vine-ripened tomatoes

4 tablespoons olive oil

1 tablespoon lemon juice

1½ tablespoons red wine vinegar

6 anchovy fillets, finely chopped

1 tablespoon baby capers, rinsed,
squeezed dry and finely chopped

1 garlic clove, crushed

3 handfuls basil

1 Preheat the oven to 220°C (425°F/Gas 7). Tear the bread into 2 cm (¾ inch) pieces, spread on a baking tray and bake for 5–7 minutes, or until golden on the outside. Leave toasted bread on a wire rack to cool.

2 Score a cross in the base of each tomato. Place tomatoes in a heatproof bowl and cover with boiling water. Leave for 20 seconds, then transfer to cold water and peel the skin away from the cross. Cut four of the tomatoes in half and squeeze the juice and seeds into a bowl, reserving and chopping the flesh. Add the oil, lemon juice, vinegar, anchovies, capers and garlic to the tomato juice, and season.

3 Seed and slice the remaining tomatoes, and place in a large bowl with the reserved tomato and most of the basil. Add the dressing and toasted bread, and toss. Garnish with the remaining basil, season, and leave for at least 15 minutes. Serve at room temperature.

CHARGRILLED VEGETABLE SALAD WITH BALSAMIC

SERVES 4–6

4 baby eggplants (aubergines)

5 roma (plum) tomatoes

2 red capsicums (peppers)

1 green capsicum (pepper)

2 zucchini (courgettes)

100 ml (3½ fl oz) olive oil

12 bocconcini (fresh baby mozarella cheese)

45 g (1½ oz/½ cup) ligurian olives

1 garlic clove, finely chopped

3 teaspoons baby capers, rinsed and squeezed dry

½ teaspoon sugar

2 tablespoons balsamic vinegar

1 **Slice the eggplant** and tomatoes in half lengthways. Cut the red and green capsicums in half lengthways, remove the seeds and membrane then cut each half into three pieces. Thinly slice the zucchini on the diagonal.

2 **Preheat a chargrill pan** to hot. Add 1 tablespoon of oil and cook one-quarter of the vegetables (cook the tomatoes, cut side down, first) for 2–3 minutes, or until marked and golden. Place in a large bowl.

3 **Cook the remaining** vegetables in batches until tender, adding more oil as needed. Transfer to the bowl and add the bocconcini. Mix the olives, garlic, capers, sugar, vinegar and remaining oil (about 2 tablespoons). Pour over the salad and toss. Season with pepper.

GREEN SALAD WITH LEMON VINAIGRETTE

SERVES 6

150 g (5½ oz) baby cos (romaine) lettuce

150 g (5½ oz) small butter lettuce

50 g (2 oz) watercress

100 g (3½ oz) rocket (arugula)

DRESSING

1 tablespoon finely chopped French shallots

2 teaspoons dijon mustard

½ teaspoon sugar

1 tablespoon finely chopped basil

1 teaspoon grated lemon zest

3 teaspoons lemon juice

1 tablespoon white wine vinegar

1 tablespoon lemon oil

4 tablespoons virgin olive oil

1   Remove the outer leaves from the cos and butter lettuces and separate the core leaves. Wash in cold water, place in a colander to drain, then refrigerate. Pinch or trim the stalks from the watercress and rocket, pat dry in a tea towel (dish towel) and chill with the lettuce.

2   To make the dressing, whisk together the shallots, mustard, sugar, basil, lemon zest, lemon juice and vinegar in a bowl until well blended. Place the oils in a small jug and slowly add to the bowl in a thin stream, whisking constantly to create a smooth, creamy dressing. Season to taste with salt and pepper.

3   Place the salad greens in a large bowl. Drizzle the dressing over the salad and toss gently to coat.

TABBOULEH

SERVES 6–8

175 g (6 oz/1 cup) burghul (bulgar)

200 g (7 oz) flat-leaf (Italian) parsley, or 100 g (3½ oz) parsley and 100 g (3½ oz) rocket (arugula)

80 g (3 oz) mint

6 spring onions (scallions), finely sliced

2 tomatoes, finely chopped

DRESSING

2 large garlic cloves, finely chopped

4 tablespoons lemon juice

125 ml (4 fl oz/½ cup) extra virgin olive oil

1 **Place the burghul** in a large bowl and add enough hot water to cover. Leave to soak for 15–20 minutes or until tender. Drain well.

2 **Finely chop the parsley** and mint, and combine in a large bowl with the drained burghul, spring onion and chopped tomato.

3 **Mix the garlic** and lemon juice together in a small bowl. Whisk in the oil until it is well combined, and season to taste with salt and black pepper. Toss the dressing through the salad before serving.

Variation: Add 3 tablespoons toasted pine nuts with the burghul.

RADICCHIO WITH FIGS AND GINGER VINAIGRETTE

SERVES 4

1 radicchio

1 small curly endive lettuce (see Note)

3 oranges

½ small red onion, thinly sliced into rings

8 small green figs, quartered

2 pomegranates (optional)

DRESSING

3 tablespoons extra virgin olive oil

1 teaspoon red wine vinegar

⅛ teaspoon ground cinnamon

2 tablespoons orange juice

2 tablespoons very finely chopped glacé ginger with syrup

1 **Wash the radicchio** and curly endive leaves in cold water, and drain well. Tear any large leaves into pieces.

2 **Peel and segment** the oranges, discarding all of the pith. Place in a large bowl with the onion rings, salad leaves and figs, reserving 8 fig quarters.

3 **To make the** dressing, combine the olive **oil,** vinegar, cinnamon, orange juice and ginger in a small bowl. Season to taste with salt and pepper. Pour over the salad and toss lightly.

4 **Arrange the reserved** figs in pairs over the salad. If you are using the pomegranates, slice them in half and scoop out the seeds with a spoon. Scatter these over the salad before serving.

Note: Curly endive is also known as frisée lettuce.

Variation: A delicious alternative for this salad is to replace the oranges and orange juice with mandarins and mandarin juice when in season.

EGG SALAD WITH CREAMY DRESSING

SERVES 4

10 large eggs, at room temperature

4 tablespoons mustard cress

DRESSING

1 egg yolk

3 teaspoons lemon juice

2 teaspoons dijon mustard

70 ml (2½ fl oz) olive oil

70 ml (2½ fl oz) safflower oil

2 tablespoons chopped dill

1½ tablespoons crème fraîche or sour cream

2 tablespoons baby capers, rinsed and squeezed dry

1 Place the eggs in a large saucepan of cold water. Bring to the boil and simmer gently for 10 minutes. Drain, then cool the eggs under cold running water. Remove the shells.

2 To make the dressing, place the egg yolk, lemon juice and dijon mustard in a food processor or blender and season with salt and freshly ground black pepper. With the motor running, slowly add the combined olive oil and safflower oil, drop by drop at first. Slowly increasing the amount to a thin, steady stream as the mixture thickens. When all of the oil has been added, place the mayonnaise in a large bowl, and gently stir in the dill, crème fraîche and capers.

3 Roughly chop the eggs and fold into the mayonnaise. Transfer the salad to a serving bowl and use scissors to cut the green tips from the mustard cress. Scatter them over the salad and serve. Serve the salad on slices of toasted bruschetta, draped with smoked salmon and topped with mustard cress and extra black pepper.

COLESLAW

SERVES 8–10

½ green cabbage

¼ red cabbage

3 carrots, coarsely grated

6 radishes, coarsely grated

1 red capsicum (pepper), chopped

4 spring onions (scallions), sliced

3 tablespoons chopped parsley

250 g (9 oz/1 cup) whole-egg mayonnaise

1 Remove the hard core from the cabbages and shred the leaves with a sharp knife. Place in a large bowl and add the grated carrot, grated radish, red capsicum, spring onion and parsley to the bowl.

2 Add the mayonnaise, season to taste with salt and freshly ground black pepper and toss until well combined.

Note: Cover and refrigerate chopped vegetables for up to 3 hours before serving. Add mayonnaise just before serving.

INSALATA CAPRESE

SERVES 4

3 large vine-ripened tomatoes

250 g (9 oz) bocconcini (fresh baby mozzarella cheese)

12 basil leaves

3 tablespoons extra virgin olive oil

4 basil leaves, roughly torn, extra (optional)

1 **Slice the tomatoes** into 1 cm (½ inch) slices, to make twelve slices altogether.

2 **Slice bocconcini into** twenty-four 1 cm (½ inch) slices.

3 **Arrange tomato slices** on a serving plate, alternating them with two slices of bocconcini. Place the basil leaves between the bocconcini slices.

4 **Drizzle with the oil,** sprinkle with the basil, if desired, and season well with salt and ground black pepper.

ROAST TOMATO SALAD

SERVES 6

6 roma (plum) tomatoes

2 teaspoons capers, rinsed and squeezed dry

6 basil leaves, torn

1 tablespoon olive oil

1 tablespoon balsamic vinegar

2 garlic cloves, crushed

½ teaspoon honey

1 **Cut the tomatoes** lengthways into quarters. Place on a baking tray, skin-side-down, and cook under a hot grill (broiler) for 4–5 minutes, or until golden. Cool to room temperature and place in a bowl.

2 **Combine the capers,** basil leaves, olive oil, balsamic vinegar, garlic cloves and honey in a bowl, season with salt and freshly ground black pepper, and pour over the tomatoes. Toss gently to combine.

BEAN SALAD

SERVES 6

250 g (9 oz) green beans, trimmed
250 g (9 oz) yellow beans, trimmed
shaved parmesan cheese

DRESSING

3 tablespoons olive oil
1 tablespoon lemon juice
1 garlic clove, crushed

1 **Bring a saucepan** of lightly salted water to the boil. Add the green and yellow beans, and cook for 2 minutes, or until just tender.

2 **Plunge the beans** into cold water and drain.

3 **To make the** dressing, place the olive oil, lemon juice and garlic in a bowl, season with salt and freshly ground black pepper, and mix together well. Place the beans in a serving bowl, pour on the dressing and toss to coat. Top with the parmesan cheese and serve.

FRISÉE WITH CROUTONS AND VINAIGRETTE

SERVES 4–6

VINAIGRETTE

1 French shallot, finely chopped

1 tablespoon dijon mustard

3 tablespoons tarragon vinegar

170 ml (5 ½ fl oz/⅔ cup) extra virgin olive oil

1 tablespoon olive oil

250 g (9 oz) speck, rind removed, cut into 5 mm x 2 cm (¼ x ¾ inch) pieces

½ baguette, sliced

4 garlic cloves

1 baby frisée (curly endive), washed and dried

50 g (2 oz/½ cup) walnuts, toasted

1 For the vinaigrette, whisk together in a bowl the shallot, mustard and vinegar. Slowly add the extra virgin olive oil, whisking constantly until thickened. Set aside.

2 Heat olive oil in a large frying pan, add the speck, bread and garlic and cook over medium–high heat for 5–8 minutes, until the bread and speck are both crisp. Remove the garlic from the pan.

3 Place the frisée, bread, speck, walnuts and vinaigrette in a large bowl. Toss together well and serve.

BEEF SALAD WITH SWEET AND SOUR CUCUMBER

SERVES 4

2 Lebanese (short) cucumbers

4 teaspoons caster (superfine) sugar

4 tablespoons red wine vinegar

1 tablespoon oil

2 large or 4 small fillet steaks, cut into strips

8 spring onions (scallions), cut into pieces

2 garlic cloves, crushed

2 tablespoons ginger, grated

2 tablespoons soy sauce

4 handfuls mixed lettuce leaves

1 **Halve cucumber lengthways,** then thinly slice and put in a colander. Sprinkle with a little salt and leave for 10 minutes. This will draw out any excess moisture.

2 **Put 2 teaspoons** each of the sugar and vinegar in a bowl and stir until the sugar dissolves. Rinse the salt off, then drain the cucumber very thoroughly before dabbing it with a piece of paper towel to soak up any leftover moisture. Combine the cucumber with the vinegar mixture.

3 **Heat half the** oil in a frying pan until it is smoking. Add half the steak and fry for 1 minute. Remove from the pan and repeat with the remaining oil and steak. Return to the same pan, then add the spring onion and fry for another minute. Add garlic and ginger, toss everything around once, then add the soy sauce and remaining sugar and vinegar. Cook until the sauce turns sticky, then quickly remove from the heat.

4 **Put a handful** of lettuce leaves on four plates and divide the beef among them. Scatter some cucumber on the beef and serve the rest on the side.

BACON AND AVOCADO SALAD

SERVES 4

8 bacon slices

400 g (14 oz) green beans, trimmed and halved

300 g (10½ oz) baby English spinach leaves

2 French shallots, finely sliced

2 avocados

DRESSING

¼ teaspoon soft brown sugar

1 garlic clove, crushed

4 tablespoons olive oil

1 tablespoon balsamic vinegar

1 teaspoon sesame oil

1 **Turn on the grill** (broiler). Put the bacon on a baking tray and grill on both sides until it is nice and crisp. Leave it to cool and then break into pieces.

2 **Bring a saucepan** of water to the boil and cook the beans for 4 minutes. Drain and then hold them under cold running water for a few seconds to stop them cooking any further.

3 **Put the spinach** in a large bowl and add the beans, bacon and shallots. Halve the avocados, then cut into cubes and add them to the bowl of salad.

4 **To make the** dressing, mix the brown **sugar** and garlic in a small bowl. Add the rest of the ingredients and whisk everything together.

5 **Pour the dressing** over the salad and toss well. Grind some black pepper over the top and sprinkle with some salt.

HALOUMI AND ASPARAGUS SALAD WITH SALSA VERDE

SERVES 4

250 g (9 oz) haloumi cheese

380 g (13½ oz) small, thin asparagus
  spears

2 tablespoons garlic oil

2 handfuls mixed salad leaves

SALSA VERDE

3 tablespoons basil

1 large handful mint

3 handfuls parsley

2 tablespoons baby capers, rinsed
  and squeezed dry

1 garlic clove

2 tablespoons olive oil

1 tablespoon lemon juice

1 tablespoon lime juice

1 **Heat a chargrill** pan over medium heat. Cut the haloumi into 1 cm (½ inch) slices and cut each slice in half diagonally to make two small triangles. Brush the haloumi and asparagus with the garlic oil. Chargrill the asparagus for 1 minute or until just tender, and the haloumi until grill marks appear and it is warmed through. Keep warm.

2 **To make the salsa verde,** place the herbs, capers, garlic and oil in a food processor and blend until smooth. Add the juices, and pulse briefly.

3 **Divide the salad leaves** among four serving plates. Top with the haloumi and asparagus, and drizzle with a little salsa verde.

ARTICHOKE, PROSCIUTTO AND ROCKET SALAD

SERVES 4

4 artichokes

2 eggs, lightly beaten

3 tablespoons breadcrumbs

3 tablespoons grated parmesan cheese

olive oil, for frying

8 slices prosciutto

150 g (5½ oz) rocket (arugula), long
   stalks trimmed

shaved parmesan cheese (optional)

DRESSING

3 teaspoons white wine vinegar

1 garlic clove, crushed

1 tablespoon olive oil

1 Bring a large saucepan of water to the boil. Remove the hard, outer leaves of each artichoke, trim the stem and cut 2–3 cm (¾–1¼ inch) off the top. Cut into quarters and remove the furry 'choke'. Boil the pieces for 2 minutes, then drain.

2 Whisk the eggs in a bowl and combine the seasoned breadcrumbs and grated parmesan cheese in another bowl. Dip each artichoke quarter into the egg, then roll in the crumb mixture to coat. Fill a frying pan with olive oil to a depth of 2 cm (¾ inch) and heat over medium–high heat. Add the artichokes in batches and fry for 2–3 minutes, or until golden. Remove from the pan and drain on paper towels.

3 Heat 1 tablespoon of olive oil in a non-stick frying pan over medium–high heat. Cook the prosciutto in two batches for 2 minutes, or until crisp and golden. Remove from the pan, reserving the oil.

4 To make the dressing, combine the olive oil, vinegar and garlic with a little salt and pepper.

5 Place the rocket in a bowl, add half of the dressing and toss well. Divide the rocket, artichokes and prosciutto among four plates, and drizzle with the remaining dressing. Garnish with shaved parmesan, if desired, and sprinkle with sea salt.

PEAR AND WALNUT SALAD WITH LIME VINAIGRETTE

SERVES 4

1 small baguette, cut into 16 thin slices

oil, for brushing

1 garlic clove, cut in half

100 g (3½ oz/1 cup) walnuts

200 g ricotta cheese

400 g mixed salad leaves

2 pears, cut into 2.5 cm (1 inch) cubes, mixed with 2 tablespoons lime juice

LIME VINAIGRETTE

3 tablespoons lime juice

3 tablespoons oil

2 tablespoons raspberry vinegar

1 teaspoon salt

½ teaspoon ground black pepper

1 **Preheat the oven** to 180°C (350°F/Gas 4). Brush baguette slices with a little oil, rub with the cut side of the garlic, then place on a baking tray. Bake for 10 minutes, or until crisp and golden. Place the walnuts on a baking tray and roast them for 5–8 minutes, or until slightly browned—shake the tray to ensure even colouring. Allow to cool for 5 minutes.

2 **To make the lime vinaigrette,** whisk together the lime juice, oil, vinegar, salt and black pepper in a small bowl. Set aside until ready to use.

3 **Spread some ricotta** cheese on each bread slice, then cook under a hot grill (broiler) for 2–3 minutes, or until hot.

4 **Place the mixed salad,** pears and walnuts in a bowl, add the vinaigrette and toss through. Divide the salad among four serving bowls and serve with the ricotta cheese croutons.

ORANGE, GOAT'S CHEESE AND HAZELNUT SALAD

SERVES 4

DRESSING

20 g (1 oz) hazelnuts
1 tablespoon orange juice
1 tablespoon lemon juice
125 ml (4 fl oz/½ cup) olive oil
250 g (9 oz) watercress, well rinsed and dried
50 g (2 oz) baby English spinach leaves, well rinsed and dried
24 orange segments
300 g (10½ oz) firm goat's cheese, sliced into 4 equal portions

1 Preheat the oven to 180°C (350°F/Gas 4). Put hazelnuts on a baking tray and roast for 5–6 minutes, or until the skin turns dark brown. Wrap the hazelnuts in a clean tea towel (dish cloth) and rub them together to remove the skins.

2 Combine the nuts, orange juice, lemon juice and a pinch of salt in a food processor. With the motor running, gradually add the oil a few drops at a time. When about half the oil has been added, pour in the remainder in a steady stream.

3 Remove the stems from the watercress and place the leaves in a bowl with the spinach, orange segments and 2 tablespoons of the dressing. Toss to combine and season to taste with pepper. Arrange the salad on four plates.

4 Heat a small, non-stick frying pan over medium–high heat and brush lightly with olive oil. When hot, carefully press each slice of goat's cheese firmly into the pan and cook for 1–2 minutes, or until a crust forms on the cheese. Carefully remove the cheese from the pan and arrange over the salads, crust-side-up. Drizzle the remaining dressing over the salads.

HALOUMI WITH SALAD AND GARLIC BREAD

SERVES 4

4 firm, ripe tomatoes

1 Lebanese (short) cucumber

140 g (5 oz) rocket (arugula)

80 g (3 oz/½ cup) pitted kalamata olives

1 loaf crusty unsliced white bread

100 ml (3½ fl oz) olive oil

1 large garlic clove, cut in half

400 g (14 oz) haloumi cheese

1 tablespoon lemon juice

1 tablespoon chopped oregano

1   Preheat the oven to 180°C (350°F/Gas 4). Heat the grill (broiler) to high.

2   Cut the tomatoes and cucumber into bite-sized chunks and place in a serving dish with the rocket and olives. Mix well.

3   Slice the bread into eight 1.5 cm (⅝ inch) slices, drizzle 1½ tablespoons of the olive oil over the bread and season with salt and pepper. Grill until lightly golden, then rub each slice thoroughly with a cut side of the garlic. Wrap the bread loosely in foil and keep warm in the oven.

4   Cut the haloumi into eight slices. Heat 2 teaspoons of the oil in a shallow frying pan and fry the haloumi slices for 1–2 minutes on each side, until crisp and golden brown.

5   Whisk together the lemon juice, oregano and remaining olive oil to use as a dressing. Season, to taste. Pour half the dressing over the salad and toss well. Arrange the haloumi on top and drizzle with the dressing. Serve immediately with the warm garlic bread.

GREAT TASTES QUICK SHORT RECIPES

SCALLOP SALAD WITH SAFFRON DRESSING

SERVES 4

DRESSING

pinch of saffron threads

3 tablespoons mayonnaise

1½ tablespoons cream

1 teaspoon lemon juice

20 scallops (500 g/1 lb 3 oz) with roe attached

2 tablespoons butter

1 tablespoon olive oil

100 g (3½ oz) mixed salad leaves

4 tablespoons chervil leaves

1 **To make the dressing,** place the saffron threads in a bowl and soak in 2 teaspoons of hot water for 10 minutes. Add the mayonnaise, mixing well, until it is a rich yellow in colour. Stir in the cream, then the lemon juice. Refrigerate until needed.

2 **Make sure the scallops** are clean of digestive tract before cooking. Heat the butter and olive oil in a large frying pan over high heat and sear the scallops in small batches for 1 minute on each side.

3 **Divide the mixed salad leaves** and chervil among four serving plates, then top each with five scallops. Drizzle the dressing over the scallops and the salad leaves before serving.

THAI MARINATED OCTOPUS SALAD

SERVES 4

8 baby octopus or 4 large octopus, cut in half (about 380 g/13½ oz)

250 ml (9 fl oz/1 cup) sweet chilli sauce

2 tablespoons lime juice

1 lemon grass stem, trimmed and finely chopped

2 Lebanese (short) cucumbers

50 g (2 oz) butter lettuce, torn into rough pieces

50 g (2 oz/1 cup) coriander (cilantro), with stalks

1 **Using a small knife,** carefully cut between the head and tentacles of the octopus, just below the eyes. Grasp the body of the octopus and push the beak out with your finger. Cut the eyes from the head of the octopus and discard the eye section. Carefully slit through one side, avoiding the ink sac, and scrape out the gut. Rinse under running water to remove any remaining gut.

2 **Put the octopus** in a bowl and add the chilli sauce, lime juice and lemon grass. Stir until well mixed. Cover with plastic wrap and chill for at least 4 hours.

3 **Cut the cucumbers** into 6 cm (2½ inch) lengths, scoop out the seeds and discard. Cut the cucumbers into batons.

4 **Heat a chargrill pan** until hot. Remove the octopus from the marinade, reserving the marinade, and cook for 2–3 minutes or until cooked through. Cool slightly. Arrange the lettuce and coriander around the edge of a plate, and pile the octopus in the centre.

5 **Add the remaining marinade** to the chargrill pan and heat gently for 2 minutes. Toss the cucumber through the marinade to warm, then spoon over the salad.

GRILLED TOFU SALAD WITH MISO DRESSING

SERVES 4

4 tablespoons light soy sauce

2 teaspoons oil, plus 2 teaspoons, extra

2 garlic cloves, crushed

1 teaspoon grated ginger

1 teaspoon chilli paste

½ teaspoon salt

500 g (1 lb 2 oz) firm tofu, cut into cubes

400 g (14 oz) mixed salad leaves

1 Lebanese (short) cucumber, finely sliced

250 g (9 oz) cherry tomatoes, halved

DRESSING

2 teaspoons white miso paste (see Note)

2 tablespoons mirin

1 teaspoon sesame oil

1 teaspoon grated ginger

1 teaspoon finely chopped chives

1 tablespoon sesame seeds, toasted

1 **Combine the tamari,** oil, garlic, ginger, chilli paste and salt in a bowl. Add the tofu and mix until well coated. Marinate for at least 10 minutes, or preferably overnight. Drain and reserve the marinade.

2 **To make the dressing,** combine the miso with 125 ml (4 fl oz/½ cup) hot water and leave until the miso dissolves. Add the mirin, sesame oil, ginger, chives and sesame seeds and stir thoroughly until it begins to thicken.

3 **Combine the salad leaves,** cucumber and tomato in a serving bowl and leave until ready to serve.

4 **Heat the extra oil** on a chargrill. Add tofu and cook over medium heat for 4 minutes, or until golden brown. Pour on the reserved marinade and cook for 1 minute over high heat. Remove from the grill and allow to cool for 5 minutes.

5 **Add the tofu** to the salad, drizzle with the dressing and toss well.

Note: Miso is Japanese bean paste and plays an important part in the cuisine of Japan. It is commonly used in soups and dressings, on grilled (broiled) foods and also as a flavouring for pickles.

PRAWN AND FENNEL SALAD

SERVES 4

1.25 kg (2 lb 12 oz) raw large prawns (shrimp), peeled and deveined

1 large fennel bulb, thinly sliced (400 g/14 oz)

300 g (10½ oz) watercress

2 tablespoons finely chopped chives

DRESSING

125 ml (4 fl oz/½ cup) extra virgin olive oil

3 tablespoons lemon juice

1 tablespoon dijon mustard

1 large garlic clove, finely chopped

1 **Bring a saucepan** of water to the boil, then add the prawns, return to the boil and simmer for 2 minutes, or until the prawns turn pink and are cooked through. Drain and leave to cool. Pat the prawns dry with paper towels and slice in half lengthways. Place in a large serving bowl.

2 **Add the fennel,** watercress and chives to the bowl and mix well.

3 **To make the dressing,** whisk the oil, lemon juice, mustard and garlic together until combined. Pour the dressing over the salad, season with salt and cracked black pepper and toss gently. Arrange the salad on serving plates and serve immediately.

ROASTED TOMATO AND BOCCONCINI SALAD

SERVES 6

8 roma (plum) tomatoes, halved

pinch of sugar

350 g (12 oz) cherry bocconcini (fresh baby mozarella cheese) (see Note)

175 g (6 oz) mizuna lettuce

DRESSING

125 ml (4 fl oz/½ cup) olive oil

3 tablespoons torn basil

2 tablespoons balsamic vinegar

1 Preheat the oven to 150°C (300°F/Gas 2). Place tomato, cut side up, on a rack over a baking tray lined with baking paper. Sprinkle with salt, cracked black pepper, and the sugar. Roast for 2 hours, remove from the oven and allow to cool.

2 Combine the oil and basil in a saucepan, and stir gently over medium heat for 3–5 minutes, or until it is very hot, but not smoking. Remove from the heat and discard the basil. Mix 2 tablespoons of oil with the vinegar.

3 Toss together the tomato, bocconcini and lettuce. Arrange the salad in a shallow serving bowl and drizzle with the dressing. Sprinkle with sea salt and cracked black pepper.

Notes: If cherry bocconcini are unavailable, use regular bocconcini cut into quarters.

Leftover basil oil can be stored in a clean jar in the refrigerator, and is great in pasta sauces.

SOMEN NOODLE SALAD WITH SESAME DRESSING

SERVES 4

SESAME DRESSING

4 tablespoons sesame seeds, toasted

2½ tablespoons light soy sauce

2 tablespoons rice vinegar

2 teaspoons sugar

½ teaspoon grated ginger

½ teaspoon dashi granules

125 g (4½ oz) dried somen noodles

100 g (3½ oz) snow peas (mangetout), finely sliced on the diagonal

100 g (3½ oz) daikon radish, julienned

100 g (1 small) carrot, cut into very thin slices

1 spring onion (scallion), sliced on the diagonal

50 g (2 oz) baby English spinach leaves, trimmed

2 teaspoons sesame seeds, toasted

1   To make the dressing, place the sesame seeds in a mortar and pestle and grind until fine and moist. Combine the soy sauce, rice vinegar, sugar, ginger, dashi granules and 125 ml (4 fl oz/½ cup) water in a small saucepan and bring to the boil over high heat. Reduce the heat to medium and simmer, stirring, for 2 minutes, or until the dashi granules have dissolved. Remove from the heat. Cool. Gradually combine with the ground sesame seeds, stirring to form a thick dressing.

2   Cook the noodles in a large saucepan of boiling water for 2 minutes, or until tender. Drain, rinse under cold water and cool completely. Cut into 10 cm (4 inch) lengths using scissors.

3   Place the snow peas in a large shallow bowl with the daikon, carrot, spring onion, English spinach leaves and the noodles. Add the dressing and toss well to combine. Place in the refrigerator until ready to serve. Just before serving, sprinkle the top with the toasted sesame seeds.

WILD RICE SALAD

SERVES 4

95 g (3¼ oz/½ cup) wild rice

250 ml (9 fl oz/1 cup) chicken stock

1 tablespoon butter

100 g (3½ oz/½ cup) basmati rice

2 bacon slices, chopped and cooked

110 g (4 oz/¾ cup) currants

60 g (2 oz/½ cup) slivered almonds, toasted

30 g (1 oz/1 cup) chopped parsley

6 spring onions (scallions), thinly sliced

grated zest and juice of 1 lemon

olive oil, to drizzle

lemon wedges, to serve

1 **Put wild rice** and stock in a saucepan, add butter, bring to the boil, then cook, covered, over low heat for 1 hour. Drain.

2 **Meanwhile, put basmati** rice in a separate pan with cold water and bring to the boil. Cook at a simmer for 12 minutes, then drain. Mix with the cooked wild rice and cool.

3 **Combine the rice** with the bacon, currants, almonds, parsley, spring onion and lemon zest and juice. Season, drizzle with olive oil and serve with lemon wedges.

PRAWN, MANGO AND MACADAMIA SALAD

SERVES 4–6

1 radicchio heart

1 large handful basil, torn

30 g (1 oz/1 cup) watercress sprigs

24 cooked king prawns (shrimp), peeled and deveined with tails intact

3 tablespoons macadamia oil

3 tablespoons extra virgin olive oil

150 g (5½ oz/1 cup) macadamia nuts, coarsely chopped

2 garlic cloves, crushed

3 tablespoons lemon juice

1 ripe mango, cut into small dice

1 Remove the outer green leaves from the radicchio, leaving only the tender pink leaves. Tear any large leaves in half and arrange in a shallow serving bowl. Scatter with half of the basil leaves and the watercress, and toss lightly. Arrange the prawns over the salad leaves.

2 Heat the oils in a small, frying pan over medium heat. Add the nuts and cook for 5 minutes, or until golden. Add the garlic and cook for a further 30 seconds, then remove from the heat and add the lemon juice and mango. Season to taste, pour over the salad and scatter with the remaining basil leaves.

VIETNAMESE PRAWN SALAD

SERVES 6

1 small Chinese cabbage, finely shredded

1 small red onion, thinly sliced

750 g (1 lb 10 oz) fresh cooked tiger prawns (shrimp), peeled and deveined, tails intact

30 g (1 oz/⅔ cup) chopped coriander (cilantro) leaves

30 g (1 oz/⅔ cup) chopped Vietnamese mint leaves (see Note)

DRESSING

3 tablespoons sugar

3 tablespoons fish sauce

4 tablespoons lime juice

1 tablespoon white vinegar

½ teaspoon salt

1 Place the Chinese cabbage in a large bowl, cover with plastic wrap and chill for 30 minutes.

2 To make the dressing put the sugar, fish sauce, lime juice, vinegar and salt in a small bowl and mix well.

3 Toss together the shredded cabbage, onion, prawns, coriander, mint and dressing, and garnish with the extra mint leaves.

Note: Vietnamese mint is available from Asian grocery stores.

SCALLOPS, GINGER AND SPINACH SALAD

SERVES 4

300 g (10½ oz) scallops, without roe

100 g (3½ oz/2 cups) baby English
    spinach leaves

1 small red capsicum (pepper), cut into
    very fine strips

50 g (2 oz) bean sprouts

DRESSING

1 tablespoon sake

1 tablespoon lime juice

2 teaspoons shaved palm sugar
    (jaggery) or soft brown sugar

1 teaspoon fish sauce

1 **Remove any membrane** or hard white muscle from
the scallops. Lightly brush a chargrill plate with oil. Cook the
scallops in batches on the chargrill plate for 1 minute each
side, or until cooked.

2 **Divide the spinach,** capsicum and bean sprouts among
four plates. Arrange the scallops over the top.

3 **To make the dressing,** place the sake, lime juice, palm
sugar and fish sauce in a small bowl, and mix together well.
Pour over the salad and serve immediately.

ASIAN TOFU SALAD

SERVES 4–6

1 large red capsicum (pepper)

1 large green capsicum (pepper)

180 g (6 oz/2 cups) bean sprouts

4 spring onions (scallions), sliced diagonally

3 tablespoons chopped coriander (cilantro)

450 g (1 lb/3 cups) shredded Chinese cabbage

3 tablespoons chopped peanuts, toasted

450 g (1 lb) firm tofu

3 tablespoons peanut oil

DRESSING

2 tablespoons sweet chilli sauce

2 tablespoons lime juice

½ teaspoon sesame oil

1½ tablespoons light soy sauce

1 garlic clove, finely chopped

3 teaspoons finely grated ginger

3 tablespoons peanut oil

1 Thinly slice the capsicums, and combine with the bean sprouts, spring onion, coriander, cabbage and peanuts.

2 Drain the liquid from the tofu and cut into 8 x 2 cm (3¼ x ¾ in) wide slices. Heat the oil in a large, frying pan. Cook the tofu for 2–3 minutes on each side, or until it is golden with a crispy edge, and add to the salad.

3 To make the dressing, mix together the chilli sauce, lime juice, sesame oil, soy, garlic and ginger. Whisk in the peanut oil, then toss through the salad and serve immediately.

MINCED PORK AND NOODLE SALAD

SERVES 4

1 tablespoon peanut oil

500 g (1 lb 2 oz) minced (ground) pork

2 garlic cloves, finely chopped

1 lemon grass stem, finely chopped

2–3 red Asian shallots, thinly sliced

3 teaspoons finely grated ginger

1 small red chilli, finely chopped

5 makrut (kaffir lime) leaves, very finely shredded

170 g (6 oz) glass (mung bean) noodles

60 g (2 oz) baby English spinach leaves

60 g (2 oz/1 cup) roughly chopped coriander (cilantro)

170 g (6 oz) peeled, finely chopped fresh pineapple

1 large handful mint leaves

DRESSING

1½ tablespoons shaved palm sugar (jaggery) or soft brown sugar

2 tablespoons fish sauce

4 tablespoons lime juice

2 teaspoons sesame oil

2 teaspoons peanut oil, extra

1 Heat a wok until very hot, add the peanut oil and swirl to coat the wok. Add the pork and stir-fry in batches over high heat for 5 minutes, or until lightly golden. Add the garlic, lemon grass, shallots, grated ginger, chilli and lime leaves, and stir-fry for a further 1–2 minutes, or until fragrant.

2 Place the noodles in a large bowl and cover with boiling water for 30 seconds, or until softened. Rinse under cold water and drain well. Toss in a bowl with the spinach, coriander, pineapple, mint and pork mixture.

3 To make the dressing, mix together the palm sugar, fish sauce and lime juice. Add the sesame oil and extra peanut oil, and whisk to combine. Toss through the salad and season with freshly ground black pepper.

SPICY LAMB AND NOODLE SALAD

SERVES 4

1 tablespoon five-spice powder

3 tablespoons vegetable oil

2 garlic cloves, crushed

2 lamb backstraps or fillets (about 250 g/9 oz each)

500 g (1 lb 2 oz) fresh Shanghai (wheat) noodles

1½ teaspoons sesame oil

80 g (3 oz) snow pea (mangetout) sprouts

½ red capsicum (pepper), thinly sliced

4 spring onions (scallions), thinly sliced on the diagonal

2 tablespoons sesame seeds, toasted

DRESSING

1 tablespoon finely chopped ginger

1 tablespoon Chinese black vinegar

1 tablespoon Chinese rice wine

2 tablespoons peanut oil

2 teaspoons chilli oil

1 Combine the five-spice powder, 2 tablespoons of the vegetable oil and garlic in a large bowl. Add the lamb and turn to coat well. Cover and marinate for 30 minutes.

2 Cook the noodles in a large saucepan of boiling water for 4–5 minutes, or until tender. Drain, rinse with cold water and drain again. Add the sesame oil and toss to combine.

3 Heat the remaining vegetable oil in a large frying pan. Cook the lamb over medium–high heat for 3 minutes each side for medium–rare, or until cooked to your liking. Rest for 5 minutes, then thinly slice across the grain.

4 To make the dressing, combine the ginger, Chinese black vinegar, rice wine, peanut oil and chilli oil.

5 Place the noodles, lamb strips, snow pea sprouts, capsicum, spring onion and the dressing in a large bowl and toss gently until well combined. Sprinkle with the sesame seeds and serve immediately.

INDIAN MARINATED CHICKEN SALAD

SERVES 4

3 tablespoons lemon juice

1½ teaspoons garam masala

1 teaspoon ground turmeric

1 tablespoon finely grated ginger

2 garlic cloves, finely chopped

3½ tablespoons vegetable oil

3 boneless, skinless chicken breasts
(650 g/1 lb 7 oz)

1 onion, thinly sliced

2 zucchini (courgettes), thinly sliced on
the diagonal

100 g (3½ oz) watercress leaves

150 g (5½ oz) freshly shelled peas

2 ripe tomatoes, finely chopped

30 g (1 oz/1 cup) coriander (cilantro)
leaves

DRESSING

1 teaspoon cumin seeds

½ teaspoon coriander seeds

4 tablespoons natural yoghurt

2 tablespoons chopped mint

2 tablespoons lemon juice

1 Combine lemon juice, garam masala, turmeric, ginger, garlic and 2 teaspoons oil in a large bowl. Add the chicken and onion, toss to coat in marinade. Cover; refrigerate for 1 hour.

2 Remove and discard the onion then heat 2 tablespoons of oil in a large, frying pan. Cook chicken for about 5 minutes on each side, or until it is cooked through. Remove chicken from the pan and leave for 5 minutes. Cut each breast across the grain into 1 cm (½ inch) slices.

3 Heat the remaining oil in the pan and cook the zucchini for 2 minutes, or until lightly golden and tender. Toss with the watercress in a large bowl. Cook the peas in boiling water for 5 minutes, or until tender, then drain. Rinse under cold water to cool. Add to the salad with the tomato, chicken and coriander.

4 For the dressing, gently roast the cumin and coriander seeds in a dry frying pan for 1–2 minutes, or until fragrant. Remove, then pound the seeds to a powder. Mix with the yoghurt, mint and lemon juice, then gently fold through the salad.

LAMB, CAPSICUM AND CUCUMBER SALAD

1 red onion, very thinly sliced

1 red capsicum (pepper), very thinly sliced

1 green capsicum (pepper), very thinly sliced

2 large Lebanese (short) cucumbers, cut into batons

4 tablespoons shredded mint

3 tablespoons chopped dill

3 tablespoons olive oil

600 g (1 lb 5 oz) lamb backstraps or fillets

DRESSING

4 tablespoons lemon juice

2 small garlic cloves, crushed

100 ml (3½ fl oz) extra virgin olive oil

1 **Combine the onion,** red and green capsicum, cucumber, mint and dill in a large bowl.

2 **Heat a chargrill pan** or frying pan until hot. Drizzle with the oil and cook the lamb for 2–3 minutes on each side, or until it is tender but still a little pink. Remove from the pan and allow to rest for 5 minutes. Thinly slice the lamb and add to the salad, tossing to mix.

3 **Combine the lemon juice** and garlic in a small bowl, then whisk in the extra virgin olive oil with a fork until well combined. Season with salt and black pepper, then toss the dressing gently through the salad.

Note: This salad is delicious served on fresh or toasted Turkish bread spread with hummus.

CHILLI CHICKEN AND CASHEW SALAD

SERVES 4

3 tablespoons sweet chilli sauce

2 tablespoons lime juice

2 teaspoons fish sauce

2 tablespoons chopped coriander (cilantro)

1 garlic clove, crushed

1 small red chilli, finely chopped

1½ teaspoons grated ginger

2 tablespoons olive oil

600 g (1 lb 5 oz) boneless, skinless chicken breasts

100 g (3½ oz) salad leaves

250 g (9 oz) cherry tomatoes, halved

100 g (3½ oz) Lebanese (short) cucumber, cut into bite-sized chunks

50 g (2 oz) snow pea (mangetout) sprouts, trimmed

80 g (3 oz/½ cup) cashew nuts, roughly chopped

1 Combine the chilli sauce, lime juice, fish sauce, coriander, garlic, chilli, ginger and 1 tablespoon of the oil in a large bowl.

2 Heat the remaining oil in a frying or chargrill pan over medium heat until hot, and cook the chicken for 5–8 minutes on each side or until cooked through. While still hot, slice each breast widthways into 1 cm (½ in) slices and toss in the bowl with the dressing. Leave to cool slightly.

3 Combine the salad leaves, cherry tomatoes, cucumber chunks and snow pea sprouts in a serving bowl. Add the chicken and all of the dressing, and toss gently until the leaves are lightly coated. Scatter with chopped cashews and serve.

ROAST DUCK SALAD WITH CHILLI DRESSING

SERVES 4–6

DRESSING

½ teaspoon chilli flakes

2½ tablespoons fish sauce

1 tablespoon lime juice

2 teaspoons grated palm sugar (jaggery) or soft brown sugar

1 Chinese roasted duck

1 small red onion, thinly sliced

1 tablespoon julienned ginger

4 tablespoons roughly chopped coriander (cilantro)

2 tablespoons roughly chopped mint

80 g (3 oz/½ cup) roasted cashews

80 g (3 oz) butter lettuce

1 **To make the dressing**, place the chilli flakes in a frying pan and dry-fry for 30 seconds, then grind to a powder in a mortar and pestle or spice grinder. Combine the chilli with the fish sauce, lime juice and palm sugar in a bowl, and set aside.

2 **Remove the flesh** from the duck and cut it into bite-sized pieces. Place the duck in a bowl with the onion, ginger, coriander, mint and cashews. Pour in the dressing and toss gently.

3 **Place the lettuce** on a serving platter. Top with the duck salad and serve.

WARM CHICKEN AND PASTA SALAD

SERVES 4

375 g (13 oz) penne

100 ml (3½ fl oz) olive oil

4 long, thin eggplants (aubergines), thinly sliced on the diagonal

2 boneless, skinless chicken breasts

2 teaspoons lemon juice

1 large handful flat-leaf (Italian) parsley, chopped

270 g (9½ oz) chargrilled red capsicum (pepper), drained and sliced

155 g (5½ oz) fresh asparagus spears, trimmed, blanched and cut into 5 cm (2 in) lengths

85 g (3 oz) semi-dried (sun-blushed) tomatoes, finely sliced

grated parmesan cheese (optional)

1 Cook the pasta in a large saucepan of boiling water until al dente. Drain, return to the pan and keep warm. Heat 2 tablespoons of the oil in a large frying pan over high heat and cook the eggplant for 4–5 minutes, or until golden and cooked through.

2 Heat a lightly oiled chargrill pan over high heat and cook the chicken for 5 minutes each side, or until browned and cooked through. Cut into thick slices. Combine the lemon juice, parsley and the remaining oil in a small jar and shake well. Return the pasta to the heat, toss through the dressing, chicken, eggplant, capsicum, asparagus and tomato until well mixed and warmed through. Season with black pepper. Serve warm with a scattering of grated parmesan cheese, if desired.

Note: Jars of chargrilled capsicum can be bought at the supermarket; otherwise, visit your local deli.

GREEK PEPPERED LAMB SALAD

SERVES 4

300 g (10½ oz) lamb backstraps or fillets

1½ tablespoons black pepper

3 vine-ripened tomatoes, cut into 8 wedges

2 Lebanese (short) cucumbers, sliced

150 g (5½ oz) lemon and garlic marinated kalamata olives, drained (reserving 1½ tablespoons oil)

100 g (3½ oz) Greek feta cheese, cubed

¾ teaspoon dried oregano

1 tablespoon lemon juice

1 tablespoon extra virgin olive oil

1 Roll the backstraps in the pepper, pressing the pepper on with your fingers. Cover and refrigerate for 15 minutes.

2 Place the tomato, cucumber, olives, feta and ½ teaspoon of the dried oregano in a bowl.

3 Heat a chargrill pan or barbecue plate, brush with oil and when very hot, cook the lamb for 2–3 minutes on each side, or until cooked to your liking. Keep warm.

4 Whisk the lemon juice, extra virgin olive oil, reserved kalamata oil and the remaining dried oregano together well. Season. Pour half the dressing over the salad, toss together and arrange on a serving platter.

5 Cut the lamb on the diagonal into 1 cm (½ in) thick slices and arrange on top of the salad. Pour the remaining dressing on top and serve.

ASIAN PORK SALAD

SERVES 4

DRESSING

2 teaspoons rice vinegar

1 small red chilli, finely chopped

2 tablespoons light soy sauce

1 teaspoon very thinly sliced ginger

¼ teaspoon sesame oil

1 star anise

2 teaspoons lime juice

250 g (9 oz) Chinese roasted pork
(char siu)

100 g (3½ oz) snow pea (mangetout)
sprouts

2 spring onions (scallions), thinly sliced
on the diagonal

½ red capsicum (pepper), thinly sliced

1   To make the dressing, combine the vinegar, chilli, soy sauce, ginger, sesame oil, star anise and lime juice in a small saucepan. Gently warm for 2 minutes, or until just about to come to the boil, then set aside to cool. Once it is cool, remove the star anise.

2   Thinly slice the pork and place in a serving bowl. Pick over the sprouts, discarding any brown or broken ones, and add to the pork. Add the spring onion and capsicum, pour on the dressing, and toss well.

SPINACH WITH CHICKEN AND SESAME DRESSING

SERVES 4

450 g (1 lb) baby English spinach leaves

1 Lebanese (short) cucumber, peeled and diced

4 spring onions (scallions), shredded

2 carrots, cut into matchsticks

2 boneless, skinless chicken breasts, cooked

2 tablespoons sesame seeds

1 large handful coriander (cilantro) leaves

DRESSING

2 tablespoons tahini

2 tablespoons lime juice

3 teaspoons sesame oil

1 teaspoon sugar

pinch of chilli flakes

1 **Put the spinach** in a large bowl. Scatter the cucumber, spring onion and carrot over the top. Shred the chicken breast into long pieces and scatter it over the vegetables.

2 **To make the dressing**, mix together the tahini, lime juice, sesame oil, sugar and chilli flakes, then add salt to taste.

3 **Cook the sesame seeds** in a dry frying pan over low heat for a minute or two, stirring them around. When they start to brown and smell toasted, tip them over the salad. Scatter the coriander leaves over the top. Drizzle on the dressing just before serving and toss the salad to combine.

4 **Toss the salad** together just before serving.

DESSERTS

MACAROON BERRY TRIFLE

SERVES 4

420 ml (14½ fl oz/1⅔ cups) skim milk

2 tablespoons caster (superfine) sugar

1 teaspoon natural vanilla extract

2½ tablespoons custard powder
    (instant vanilla pudding mix)

1 tablespoon Marsala

2 teaspoons instant coffee powder

16 amaretti biscuits (cookies), roughly
    broken

2 tablespoons orange juice

200 g (7 oz) fresh raspberries

425 g (15 oz) tin pears in natural juice,
    drained, roughly chopped

vanilla ice cream

1 Place milk, sugar and vanilla in a heavy-based saucepan and cook over low heat, stirring occasionally. Combine the custard powder with 2 tablespoons of water, mix to a smooth paste and whisk into the milk mixture until the custard boils and thickens. Remove from the heat and cover with plastic wrap, placing it directly on the surface of the custard to prevent any skin forming, and allow to cool.

2 Place the Marsala and coffee powder in a small bowl and stir until the coffee has dissolved. Place the biscuits and orange juice in a large bowl and stir to coat the biscuits. Layer half of the biscuit in the base of four serving glasses and drizzle with the Marsala mixture. Top with one-third of the berries and half of the pear, then pour in half of the custard. Repeat the layering, finishing with the raspberries. Refrigerate the trifles for 10 minutes or serve at once with vanilla ice cream.

LEMON GRASS AND GINGER-INFUSED FRUIT SALAD

SERVES 4

3 tablespoons caster (superfine) sugar

2 x 2 cm (¾ x ¾ in) piece fresh ginger, thinly sliced

1 lemon grass stem, bruised and halved

1 large passionfruit

1 red pawpaw

½ honeydew melon

1 large mango

1 small fresh pineapple

12 fresh lychees

3 tablespoons mint leaves, shredded

1 Place the sugar, ginger and lemon grass in a small saucepan, add 125 ml (4 fl oz/½ cup) water and stir over low heat to dissolve the sugar. Boil for 5 minutes, or until reduced to 4 tablespoons, and cool. Strain the syrup and add the passionfruit pulp.

2 Peel and seed the pawpaw and melon. Cut into 4 cm (1½ in) cubes. Peel the mango and cut the flesh into cubes, discarding the stone. Peel, halve and core the pineapple and cut into cubes. Peel the lychees, then make a slit in the flesh and remove the seed.

3 Place all the fruit in a large serving bowl. Pour on the syrup, or serve separately if preferred. Garnish with the shredded mint.

PEACHES POACHED IN WINE

SERVES 4

4 just-ripe yellow-fleshed freestone peaches

500 ml (17 fl oz/2 cups) dessert wine such as Sauternes

3 tablespoons orange liqueur

220 g (7½ oz/1 cup) sugar

1 cinnamon stick

1 vanilla bean, split

8 mint leaves

mascarpone cheese or crème fraîche

1   Cut a small cross in the base of each peach. Immerse the peaches in boiling water for 30 seconds, then drain and cool slightly. Peel off the skin, cut in half and carefully remove the stones.

2   Place the wine, liqueur, sugar, cinnamon stick and vanilla bean in a deep-sided frying pan large enough to hold the peach halves in a single layer. Heat the mixture, stirring, until the sugar dissolves. Bring to the boil, then reduce the heat and simmer for 5 minutes. Add the peaches to the pan and simmer for 4 minutes, turning them over halfway through. Remove with a slotted spoon and leave to cool. Continue to simmer the syrup for 6–8 minutes, or until thick. Strain and set aside.

3   Arrange the peaches on a serving platter, cut side up. Spoon the syrup over the top and garnish each half with a mint leaf. Serve the peaches warm or chilled, with a dollop of mascarpone or crème fraîche.

STRAWBERRIES WITH BALSAMIC VINEGAR

SERVES 4

750 g (1 lb 10 oz) ripe small strawberries

3 tablespoons caster (superfine) sugar

2 tablespoons balsamic vinegar

125 g (4½ oz/½ cup) mascarpone

1 Wipe the strawberries with a clean damp cloth and carefully remove the green stalks. If the strawberries are large, cut each one in half.

2 Place all the strawberries in a large glass bowl, sprinkle the caster sugar evenly over the top and toss gently to coat. Set aside for 2 hours to macerate, then sprinkle the balsamic vinegar over the strawberries. Toss them again, then refrigerate for about 30 minutes.

3 Spoon the strawberries into four glasses, drizzle with syrup and top with a dollop of mascarpone.

Note: If you leave the strawberries for more than 2 hours, it is best to refrigerate them.

ETON MESS

SERVES 4

4–6 ready-made meringues

250 g (9 oz) strawberries

1 teaspoon caster (superfine) sugar

250 ml (9 fl oz/1 cup) thick (double/
heavy) cream

1 Break the meringues into pieces. Cut the strawberries into quarters and put them in a bowl with the sugar. Using a potato masher or the back of a spoon, squash them slightly so they start to become juicy.

2 Whip the cream with a balloon or electric whisk until it is quite thick but not solid.

3 Mix everything together gently and spoon it into glasses.

DRIED APRICOT FOOL

SERVES 4

30 g (1 oz) finely chopped glacé ginger

175 g (6 oz/1 cup) dried apricots, chopped

2 egg whites

2 tablespoons caster (superfine) sugar

1 tablespoon shredded coconut, toasted

1 Place the ginger, apricots and 4 tablespoons water in a small saucepan. Cook, covered, over very low heat for 5 minutes, stirring occasionally. Remove from the heat and allow to cool completely.

2 Using electric beaters, beat the egg whites in a clean, dry bowl until soft peaks form. Add the caster sugar and beat for 3 minutes, or until thick and glossy. Quickly and gently fold the cooled apricot mixture into the egg mixture and divide among four chilled serving glasses. Scatter the coconut over the top and serve immediately.

Note: The apricots can scorch easily, so cook over low heat. Serve immediately, or the egg white will slowly break down and lose volume.

WINTER FRUIT IN ORANGE GINGER SYRUP

SERVES 4

3 tablespoons caster (superfine) sugar

3 tablespoons orange juice

2 strips orange rind

1 cinnamon stick

250 g (9 oz) dried fruit salad, large
    pieces cut in half

100 g (3½ oz) pitted dried dates

1 teaspoon grated ginger

200 g (7 oz) plain yoghurt

1 **Place the caster sugar,** orange juice, orange rind, cinnamon stick and 375 ml (13 fl oz/1½ cups) water in a large saucepan. Stir over low heat until the caster sugar dissolves, then increase the heat and simmer, without stirring, for 5 minutes, or until the syrup mixture has thickened slightly.

2 **Add the dried fruit** salad, dates and ginger, and toss well. Cover and simmer over low heat for 5 minutes, or until the fruit has softened. Remove from the heat and set aside, covered, for 5 minutes. Discard the orange rind and cinnamon stick. If serving cold, remove from the saucepan and allow to cool.

3 **Place the fruits** in individual serving dishes, top with the yoghurt and drizzle a little of the syrup over the top.

FRUIT POACHED IN RED WINE

SERVES 6

3 pears, peeled, quartered and cored

3 apples, peeled, quartered and cored

50 g (2 oz) sugar

1 vanilla bean, cut in half lengthways

2 small cinnamon sticks

400 ml (14 fl oz) red wine

200 ml (7 fl oz) dessert wine or port

700 g (1 lb 9 oz) red-skinned plums, halved

1 **Put the pears** and apples in a large saucepan. Add sugar, vanilla bean, cinnamon sticks, red wine and dessert wine and bring to the boil. Reduce the heat and gently simmer for about 5–10 minutes, or until just soft.

2 **Add the plums**, stirring them through the pears and apples, and bring the liquid back to a simmer. Cook for another 5 minutes, or until the plums are soft.

3 **Remove the saucepan** from heat, cover with a lid and leave the fruit to marinate in the syrup for at least 6 hours. Reheat gently to serve warm or serve at room temperature with cream or ice cream and a biscuit (cookie).

BANANA SOY PANCAKES WITH HONEYCOMB BUTTER

SERVES 4

HONEYCOMB BUTTER ·
4 tablespoons butter, softened

1 tablespoon honey

60 g (2 oz) crushed honeycomb

PANCAKES
2 bananas

325–375 ml (11–13 fl oz) vanilla soy milk

2 eggs

1 tablespoon caster (superfine) sugar

30 g (1 oz) butter, melted

1 teaspoon natural vanilla extract

225 g (7½ oz/1½ cups) self-raising flour

½ teaspoon bicarbonate of soda (baking soda)

icing (confectioners') sugar, to garnish

ice cream, to serve

1 **To make the honeycomb** butter, beat the butter and honey together, then fold through the crushed honeycomb.

2 **To make the pancakes,** cut one of the bananas into pieces and put in a blender. Add three-quarters of the soy milk, the eggs, sugar, melted butter and vanilla. Whizz for 10–15 seconds, or until the batter is smooth. Add the remaining soy milk a little at a time.

3 **Add the flour** and bicarbonate of soda and whizz in short bursts for 30 seconds, or until well combined and smooth. Pour the batter into a pitcher. Thinly slice the remaining banana and stir it into the batter.

4 **Heat a large** non-stick frying pan over medium heat and lightly grease with melted butter. Pour 3 tablespoons of the batter into the pan and cook for 2 minutes, or until bubbles appear on the surface. Turn and cook for 2 minutes or until cooked and golden. Transfer the pancake to a wire rack and cover with a tea towel (dish towel) to keep warm while you cook the remaining pancakes.

5 **Serve the pancakes** dusted with icing sugar and topped with a small scoop of ice cream and the honeycomb butter.

PASSIONFRUIT CREAM WITH SNAP BISCUITS

SERVES 6–8

SNAP BISCUITS (COOKIES)

100 g (3½ oz/⅔ cup) blanched almonds

115 g (4 oz/½ cup) caster (superfine) sugar

60 g (2¼ oz) unsalted butter, softened

1 tablespoon plain (all-purpose) flour

1 egg white

8 passionfruit

125 g (4½ oz/1 cup) raspberries

250 g (9 oz/1 cup) ricotta cheese

60 g (2 oz/½ cup) icing (confectioners') sugar, sifted, plus extra for dusting

½ teaspoon natural vanilla extract

150 ml (5 fl oz) cream, whipped

1 To make the snap biscuits, preheat the oven to 180°C (350°F/Gas 4). Line two baking trays with baking paper.

2 Put the almonds and half the caster sugar in a small processor fitted with the metal blade and whizz for 1 minute, or until a fine powder forms. Add the remaining sugar, the butter, flour and egg white and whizz until just combined.

3 Drop rounded teaspoons of mixture 5 cm (2 inches) apart onto one of the prepared baking trays and flatten them with the back of a spoon. Bake for 7–8 minutes, or until golden. Remove from the oven and slide the paper with the biscuits onto a flat surface to cool. Repeat with the remaining mixture.

4 Halve six of the passionfruit and strain the juice through a fine sieve into a bowl. Discard the pulp. Halve the remaining passionfruit, scoop pulp into a bowl. Gently stir in raspberries, reserving a few for garnish. Cover and chill until needed.

5 Put ricotta, icing sugar, vanilla and strained passionfruit juice into the clean processor fitted with the plastic blade. Whizz for 30 seconds, then scrape down the side of the bowl. Repeat until the mixture is smooth. Transfer to a large bowl. Using a metal spoon, carefully fold the whipped cream through the ricotta mixture until well combined. Cover and refrigerate until needed.

6 To serve, gently fold the raspberry mixture through the passionfruit cream. Put one of the snap biscuits on each plate, spoon on the passionfruit cream, then top with another biscuit. Dust with icing sugar and garnish with the reserved raspberries. Serve immediately.

MANGO FOOL

SERVES 2

2 very ripe mangoes
250 g (9 oz/1 cup) Greek-style yoghurt
4 tablespoons cream

1 **Take the flesh** off the mangoes. The easiest way to do this is to slice down either side of the stone so you have two 'cheeks'. Make crisscross cuts through the mango flesh on each cheek, almost through to the skin, then turn each cheek inside out and slice the flesh from the skin into a bowl. Cut the rest of the flesh from the stone.

2 **Purée the flesh** by using a food processor or blender, or just mash the flesh thoroughly with a fork.

3 **Put a spoonful** of mango purée in the bottom of 2 serving glasses, put a spoonful of yoghurt on top and then repeat. Spoon the cream equally over each serving when you have used up all the mango and yoghurt. Swirl the layers together just before eating.

SPICED FRUIT SALAD

SERVES 4

110 g (4 oz/½ cup) caster (superfine) sugar

4 slices ginger

1 bird's eye chilli, cut in half

juice and zest of 2 limes

fruit, a mixture of watermelon, melon, mango, banana, cherries, lychees, kiwi fruit, or anything else you fancy—enough for 4 portions

1 **Put the sugar** in a saucepan with 125 ml (4 fl oz/½ cup) water and the ginger and chilli. Heat it until the sugar melts, then leave it to cool before adding the lime juice and zest. Take out the ginger and chilli.

2 **Put your selection** of fruit into a bowl and pour the syrup over it. Leave it to marinate in the fridge for 30 minutes.

3 **Serve with coconut** ice cream or any other kind of ice cream or sorbet.

CRÈME CARAMEL

SERVES 6

250 ml (9 fl oz/1 cup) milk

250 ml (9 fl oz/1 cup) cream

375 g (13 oz/1½ cups) caster (superfine) sugar

1 teaspoon natural vanilla extract

4 eggs, lightly beaten

4 tablespoons caster (superfine) sugar, extra

1 Preheat the oven to 200°C (400°F/Gas 6). Place the milk and cream in a saucepan and gradually bring to boiling point.

2 Put the sugar in a frying pan and cook over medium heat for 8–10 minutes. Stir occasionally as the sugar melts to form a golden toffee. The sugar may clump together—break up any lumps with a wooden spoon. Pour the toffee into the base of six 125 ml (4 fl oz/½ cup) ramekins or ovenproof dishes. Take care doing this as the toffee is very hot.

3 Combine the vanilla, eggs and extra sugar in a bowl. Remove the milk and cream from the heat and gradually add to the egg mixture, whisking well. Pour the custard mixture evenly over the toffee. Place the ramekins in a baking dish and pour in boiling water until it comes halfway up the sides of the dishes. Bake for 20 minutes, or until set. Use a flat-bladed knife to run around the edges of the dishes and carefully turn out the crème caramel onto a serving plate, toffee side up.

Note: When making toffee, watch it carefully as it will take a little while to start melting, but once it starts it will happen very quickly. Stir occasionally to make sure it melts evenly and doesn't stick to the saucepan.

GRILLED FIGS WITH RICOTTA

SERVES 4

2 tablespoons honey

1 cinnamon stick

3 tablespoons flaked almonds

4 large (or 8 small) fresh figs

125 g (4½ oz/½ cup) ricotta cheese

½ teaspoon natural vanilla extract

2 tablespoons icing (confectioners') sugar, sifted

pinch of ground cinnamon

½ teaspoon finely grated orange zest

1 Place the honey and cinnamon stick in a small saucepan with 4 tablespoons water. Bring to the boil, then reduce the heat and simmer gently for 6 minutes, or until thickened and reduced by half. Discard the cinnamon stick and stir in the almonds.

2 Preheat the grill (broiler) to moderately hot and grease a shallow ovenproof dish large enough to fit all the figs side by side. Slice the figs into quarters from the top to within 1 cm (½ inch) of the bottom, keeping them attached at the base. Arrange in the prepared dish.

3 Combine the ricotta, vanilla, icing sugar, ground cinnamon and orange zest in a small bowl. Divide the filling among the figs, spooning it into their cavities. Spoon the syrup over the top. Place under the grill and cook until the juices start to come out from the figs and the almonds are lightly toasted. Cool for 2–3 minutes. Spoon the juices and any fallen almonds from the bottom of the dish over the figs and serve.

TIRAMISU

SERVES 4

5 eggs, separated

180 g (6 oz) caster (superfine) sugar

250 g (9 oz) mascarpone cheese

250 ml (9 fl oz/1 cup) cold very strong coffee

3 tablespoons brandy or sweet Marsala

44 small sponge finger biscuits (cookies)

80 g (3 oz) dark chocolate, finely grated

1 **Beat the egg yolks** with the sugar until the sugar has dissolved and the mixture is light and fluffy and leaves a ribbon trail when dropped from the whisk. Add the mascarpone and beat until the mixture is smooth. Whisk the egg whites in a clean dry glass bowl until soft peaks form. Fold into the mascarpone mixture.

2 **Pour the coffee** into a shallow dish and add the brandy. Dip some of the sponge finger biscuits into the coffee mixture, using enough biscuits to cover the base of a 25 cm (10 inch) square dish. The biscuits should be fairly well soaked on both sides but not so much so that they break up. Arrange the biscuits in one tightly packed layer in the base of the dish.

3 **Spread half the mascarpone** mixture over the layer of biscuits. Add another layer of soaked biscuits and then another layer of mascarpone, smoothing the top layer neatly. Leave to rest in the fridge for at least 2 hours or overnight. Dust with the grated chocolate to serve.

ZUPPA INGLESE

SERVES 4

4 thick slices sponge or madeira (pound) cake

4 tablespoons kirsch

150 g (5½ oz/1¼ cups) raspberries

170 g (6 oz/1⅓ cups) blackberries

2 tablespoons caster (superfine) sugar

250 ml (9 fl oz/1 cup) custard

250 ml (9 fl oz/1 cup) cream, lightly whipped

icing (confectioners') sugar, to dust

1 **Put a piece** of sponge cake on each of four deep plates and brush or sprinkle it with the kirsch. Leave the kirsch to soak in for at least a minute or two.

2 **Put the raspberries** and blackberries in a saucepan with the caster sugar. Gently warm through over a low heat so that the sugar just melts, then leave the fruit to cool.

3 **Spoon the fruit** over the sponge, pour the custard on top and, finally, dollop the cream on top and dust with icing sugar.

PEACHES CARDINAL

SERVES 4

4 large ripe peaches

300 g (10½ oz/2½ cups) raspberries

2 tablespoons icing (confectioners')
  sugar, plus extra, to dust

1 If the peaches are very ripe, put them in a bowl and pour boiling water over them. Leave for a minute, then drain and carefully peel away the skin. If the fruit is not so ripe, dissolve 2 tablespoons sugar in a saucepan of water, add the peaches and cover pan. Gently poach peaches for 5–10 minutes, or until they are tender. Drain and peel.

2 Let the peaches cool. Halve each one and remove the stone. Put two halves in each serving glass. Put the raspberries in a food processor or blender and mix until puréed (or mix by hand). Pass through a fine nylon sieve to get rid of the seeds.

3 Sift the icing sugar over the raspberry purée and stir in. Drizzle the purée over the peaches, cover and chill thoroughly. Dust a little icing sugar over the top to serve.

CREPES WITH WARM FRUIT COMPOTE

SERVES 4

CREPES

60 g (2 oz/½ cup) plain (all-purpose) flour

2 eggs

250 ml (9 fl oz/1 cup) milk

2 teaspoons caster (superfine) sugar

COMPOTE

100 g (3½ oz/½ cup) whole dried apricots

3 tablespoons port or Muscat

1 vanilla bean, halved

2 firm pears, peeled, cored and quartered

2 cinnamon sticks

425 g (15 oz) tin pitted prunes in syrup, drained, syrup reserved

1   Place the flour in a bowl and gradually add the combined eggs and milk, whisking to remove any lumps. Cover the batter with plastic wrap and leave for 30 minutes.

2   To make the compote, put the apricots and port in a pan and cook, covered, over low heat for 2–3 minutes, or until softened. Scrape the seeds from the vanilla bean and add both the seeds and vanilla bean to the pan along with the pear, cinnamon and prune syrup. Simmer, covered, stirring occasionally, for 4 minutes, or until the pear has softened. Add the prunes and simmer for 1 minute.

3   Heat a 20 cm (8 inch) non-stick crepe pan or frying pan over medium heat. Lightly grease with oil. Pour 3 tablespoons of batter into the pan and swirl evenly over the base. Cook each crepe for 1 minute, or until the underside is golden. Turn it over and cook the other side for 30 seconds, then remove. Keep warm and repeat to make eight crepes.

4   Fold the crepes into triangles and scatter with caster sugar. Serve with the compote.

MINI ÉCLAIRS

MAKES 24

4 tablespoons unsalted butter, chopped

125 g (4½ oz/1 cup) plain flour, sifted

4 eggs, beaten

300 ml (10½ oz/1¼ cups) thick (double/heavy) cream

1 tablespoon icing (confectioners') sugar, sifted

½ teaspoon natural vanilla extract

60 g (2 oz) dark chocolate, melted

1   Preheat the oven to 200°C (400°F/Gas 6) and line two baking trays with baking paper. Put the butter in a pan with 250 ml (9 fl oz/1 cup) water. Stir over low heat until melted. Bring to the boil, then remove from the heat and add all the flour. Beat with a wooden spoon until smooth. Return to the heat and beat for 2 minutes, or until the mixture forms a ball and leaves the side of the pan. Remove from the heat and transfer to a bowl. Cool for 5 minutes. Add the egg, a little at a time, beating well between each addition, until thick and glossy—a wooden spoon should stand upright.

2   Spoon mixture into a piping bag with a 1.2 cm (½ inch) plain nozzle. Pipe 6 cm (2½ inch) lengths of batter on the trays. Bake for 10 minutes, then reduce the heat to 180°C (350°F/Gas 4) and cook for 10 minutes, or until golden and puffed. Poke a hole into one side of each éclair and remove the soft dough from inside with a teaspoon. Return to the oven for 2–3 minutes. Cool on a rack.

3   Whip cream, icing sugar and vanilla until thick. Then pipe the cream into the side of each éclair. Dip each éclair into the melted chocolate, face side down, then return to the wire rack for the chocolate to set.

GREAT TASTES QUICK SHORT RECIPES

BAKED CUSTARD

SERVES 4

1 tablespoon unsalted butter, melted
3 eggs
4 tablespoons caster (superfine) sugar
500 ml (17 fl oz/2 cups) milk
125 ml (4 fl oz/½ cup) cream
1½ teaspoons natural vanilla extract
freshly grated nutmeg

1   **Preheat oven to** 160°C (315°F/Gas 2–3) and brush four 250 ml (9 fl oz/1 cup) ramekins or a 1.5 litre (52 fl oz/6 cup) ovenproof dish with the melted butter.

2   **Whisk together the eggs** and sugar in a large bowl until they are combined. Place the milk and cream in a small saucepan and stir over medium heat for 3–4 minutes, or until the mixture is warmed through, then stir into the egg mixture with the vanilla essence. Strain into the prepared dishes and sprinkle with the grated nutmeg.

3   **Place the dishes** in a deep roasting tin and add enough hot water to come halfway up the side of the dishes. Bake for 25 minutes for the individual custards, or 30 minutes for the large custard, or until it is set and a knife inserted into the centre comes out clean.

4   **Remove the custards** from the roasting tin and leave for 10 minutes before serving.

Variation: Omit vanilla and add 1½ tablespoons of Amaretto (almond liqueur) or Grand Marnier (orange liqueur) to the custard before baking.

COCONUT LIME ICE CREAM

SERVES 4

3 tablespoons desiccated coconut

1½ tablespoons grated lime rind

4 tablespoons lime juice

4 tablespoons coconut milk powder

1 litre (35 fl oz/4 cups) good-quality vanilla ice cream, softened

coconut macaroon biscuits (cookies), to serve

1 **Combine desiccated coconut**, grated lime rind, lime juice and coconut milk powder in a bowl and mix well.

2 **Add coconut mixture** to ice cream and fold through with a large metal spoon until evenly incorporated. Work quickly so that the ice cream does not melt. Return the mixture to the freezer and freeze for 30 minutes to firm. To serve, place 3 scoops in four latté glasses and serve with some coconut macaroon biscuits on the side.

SERVES 6

4 slices of madeira (pound) cake or trifle sponges
3 tablespoons sweet sherry or Madeira
250 g (9 oz/2 cups) raspberries
4 eggs
2 tablespoons caster (superfine) sugar
2 tablespoons plain (all-purpose) flour
500 ml (17 fl oz/2 cups) milk
¼ teaspoon natural vanilla extract
125 ml (4 fl oz/½ cup) cream, whipped
3 tablespoons flaked almonds, to decorate
raspberries, to decorate

1 **Put the cake** in the base of a bowl, then sprinkle it with the sherry. Scatter the raspberries over the top and crush them gently into the sponge with the back of a spoon to release their tart flavour, leaving some of them whole.

2 **Mix eggs, sugar** and flour together in a bowl. Heat the milk in a pan, pour it over the egg mixture, stir well and pour back into a clean pan. Cook over medium heat until the custard boils and thickens and coats the back of a spoon. Stir in the vanilla, cover the surface with plastic wrap and leave to cool.

3 **Pour cooled custard** over the raspberries and leave to set in the fridge—it will firm up but not become solid. Spoon the whipped cream over the custard. Be extravagant decorating with almonds and raspberries (or anything else you fancy) and refrigerate until needed.

INDEX

A

artichoke, prosciutto and rocket salad 109
Asian pork salad 132
Asian tofu salad 123
asparagus
    asparagus with smoked salmon and eggs 18
    haloumi and asparagus salad with salsa verde 108

B

bacon
    bacon and avocado salad 107
    cheesy bubble and squeak cakes with bacon 28
    ciabatta breakfast toasts 19
    mini quiches lorraines 29
bagels with smoked salmon and caper salsa 37
banana soy pancakes with honeycomb butter 144
battered fish and chunky wedges 47
beans
    baked potatoes with cheesy broad beans 25
    bean enchiladas 33
    bean salad 104
    rice noodles with beef and black beans 56
    salmon with bean purée 66
beef
    beef salad with sweet and sour cucumber 106
    rice noodles with beef and black beans 56
    steak with maître d'hotel butter 71
    surf 'n' turf 70
berries
    Eton mess 140
    macaroon berry trifle 136
    passionfruit cream with snap biscuits 145
    strawberries with balsamic vinegar 139
    trifle 157
    zuppa inglese 151
bruschetta 13

C

Caesar salad 92
Cajun chicken with tomato and corn salsa 87
capsicum
    chicken with peach, capsicum and bean salsa 61
    fish fillets with fennel and red capsicum salsa 79
    lamb, capsicum and cucumber salad 127
cheese
    baked potatoes with cheesy broad beans 25
    barbecued haloumi 30

    cheese and chilli shapes 10
    cheesy bubble and squeak cakes with bacon 28
    chicken breast with goat's cheese 65
    crunchy cheese bites 14
    goat's cheese, leek and tapenade parcels 23
    grilled figs with ricotta 149
    haloumi and asparagus salad with salsa verde 108
    haloumi with salad and garlic bread 112
    leek, zucchini and cheese frittata 34
    mushrooms with marinated feta 24
    orange, goat's cheese and hazelnut salad 111
    orecchiette with smoked mozzarella 63
    roasted tomato and bocconcini salad 117
chicken
    Cajun chicken with tomato and corn salsa 87
    chicken breast with goat's cheese 65
    chicken with peach, capsicum and bean salsa 61
    chicken skewers with spicy chilli 46
    chicken and vegetable pasta 72
    chilli chicken and cashew salad 128
    chilli linguine with chermoula chicken 60
    crunchy chicken bits 32
    fresh spring rolls 20
    Indian marinated chicken salad 126
    paprika garlic chicken 76
    roast chicken with wild rice 50
    salt and pepper chicken with Asian greens 57
    spinach with chicken and sesame dressing 133
    steamed lemon grass and ginger chicken 81
    warm chicken and pasta salad 130
chickpea fritters 21
chilli
    cheese and chilli shapes 10
    chicken skewers with spicy chilli 46
    chilli chicken and cashew salad 128
    chilli linguine with chermoula chicken 60
    lamb cutlets with spicy yoghurt sauce 59
    roast duck salad with chilli dressing 129
ciabatta breakfast toasts 19
coconut lime ice cream 156
coleslaw 101
crème caramel 148
crepes
    banana soy pancakes with honeycomb butter 144
    crepes with warm fruit compote 153
crunchy chicken bits 32
cucumber
    lamb, capsicum and cucumber salad 127
    Thai fried prawn balls with spicy salad 42
    tzatziki 11
custard, baked 155

D

duck, roast duck salad with chilli dressing 129

E

éclairs, mini 154
eggs
    asparagus with smoked salmon and eggs 18
    classic omelette 35
    egg salad with creamy dressing 100
    scallop fritters 27
    Spanish omelette with smoked salmon 36
Eton mess 140

F

fajitas, tofu 38
farfalle with prawns and horseradish cream 55
fennel
    fish fillets with fennel and red capsicum salsa 79
    prawn and fennel salad 116
figs, grilled, with ricotta 149
fish
    battered fish and chunky wedges 47
    crispy fish and lentils 83
    fish fillets with fennel and red capsicum salsa 79
    fish rolls 78
    saffron fish cakes with herb crème fraîche 39
    see also seafood
fools
    dried apricot fool 141
    mango fool 146
frisée with croutons and vinaigrette 105
frittatas
    leek, zucchini and cheese 34
    mini sweet potato and leek 22
fritters
    chickpea 21
    scallop 27
fruit
    crepes with warm fruit compote 153
    fruit poached in red wine 143
    lemon grass and ginger infused fruit salad 137
    spiced fruit salad 147
    winter fruit in orange ginger syrup 142

G

garlic
    haloumi with salad and garlic bread 112
    paprika garlic chicken 76
ginger
    lemon grass and ginger infused fruit salad 137
    radicchio with figs and ginger vinaigrette 99
    scallops, ginger and spinach salad 122

GREAT TASTES QUICK SHORT RECIPES

steamed lemon grass with ginger chicken 81
winter fruit in orange ginger syrup 142
goat's cheese, leek and tapenade parcels 23
Greek peppered lamb salad 131
Greek salad 94
Greek-style lamb 77
green salad with lemon vinaigrette 97

H

haloumi
barbecued haloumi 30
haloumi and asparagus salad with salsa verde 108
haloumi with salad and garlic bread 112

I

ice cream, coconut lime 156
Indian marinated chicken salad 126
insalata caprese 102

J

jars, sterilising 12
john dory with prawns and creamy dill sauce 88

L

lamb
Greek peppered lamb salad 131
Greek-style lamb 77
lamb, capsicum and cucumber salad 127
lamb cutlets with spicy yoghurt sauce 59
lamb fillet with pea sauce 82
lamb koftas in pitta bread 86
rack of lamb with herb crust 64
spicy lamb and noodle salad 125
leeks
goat's cheese, leek and tapenade parcels 23
leek, zucchini and cheese frittata 34
mini sweet potato and leek frittatas 22
lemon
farfalle with prawns and lemon horseradish cream 55
lemon mustard sauce 70
lemon pepper tuna burger 41
salmon fillets with lemon hollandaise sauce 48
lemon grass
lemon grass and ginger infused fruit salad 137
steamed lemon grass and ginger chicken 81
linguine with roasted cherry tomatoes 62

M

macaroon berry trifle 136
mango fool 146
modern salad Niçoise 93
mushrooms with marinated feta 24

N

noodles
minced pork and noodle salad 124
rice noodles with beef, black beans and capsicums 56
salmon with miso and soy noodles 54
somen noodle salad with sesame dressing 118
spice-crusted salmon and noodle salad 80
spicy lamb and noodle salad 125
tuna steaks on coriander noodles 89
nuts
chilli chicken and cashew salad 128
open lasagne with rocket and walnut pesto 85
orange, goat's cheese and hazelnut salad 111
pear and walnut salad with lime vinaigrette 110
prawn, mango and macadamia salad 120

O

octopus
chargrilled baby octopus 17
Thai marinated octopus salad 114
omelettes
classic omelette 35
Spanish omelette with smoked salmon 36
stuffed prawn omelettes 68
orange, goat's cheese and hazelnut salad 111
orecchiette with smoked mozzarella 63

P

paprika garlic chicken 76
passionfruit cream with snap biscuits 145
pasta
chicken and vegetable pasta 72
chilli linguine with chermoula chicken 60
farfalle with prawns and horseradish cream 55
fresh tomato and basil sauce with pasta 53
kid's quick pasta with tomato sauce 84
linguine with roasted cherry tomatoes 62
open lasagne with rocket and walnut pesto 85
orecchiette with smoked mozzarella 63
seafood pasta 67
spaghetti carbonara 52
vegetable and veal pasta 73
warm chicken and pasta salad 130
pastry
crunchy cheese bites 14
goat's cheese, leek and tapenade parcels 23
mini quiches lorraines 29
vegetable strudels 15
peaches cardinal 152
peaches poached in wine 138

pear and walnut salad with lime vinaigrette 110
pitta pizzas 31
pork
Asian pork salad 132
minced pork and noodle salad 124
pork chops in Marsala 74
pork san choy bau 26
potatoes
baked potatoes with cheesy broad beans 25
battered fish and chunky wedges 47
saffron fish cakes with herb crème fraîche 39
prawns
farfalle with prawns and horseradish cream 55
john dory with prawns and creamy dill sauce 88
prawn, mango and macadamia salad 120
prawn cocktails 16
prawn and fennel salad 116
prawn pulao 51
stuffed prawn omelettes 68
Thai fried prawn balls with spicy salad 42
Vietnamese prawn salad 121

Q

quiches lorraines, mini 29

R

radicchio with figs and ginger vinaigrette 99
rice
prawn pulao 51
salmon kedgeree 49
salt and pepper chicken with Asian greens 57
rice noodles with beef and black beans 56

S

saffron fish cakes with herb crème fraîche 39
salads
artichoke, prosciutto and rocket salad 109
Asian pork salad 132
Asian tofu salad 123
bacon and avocado salad 107
bean salad 104
beef salad with sweet and sour cucumber 106
Caesar salad 92
chargrilled vegetable salad with balsamic 96
chilli chicken and cashew salad 128
coleslaw 101
egg salad with creamy dressing 100
frisée with croutons and vinaigrette 105
Greek peppered lamb salad 131
Greek salad 94
green salad with lemon vinaigrette 97
grilled tofu salad with miso dressing 115

haloumi and asparagus salad with salsa verde 108

haloumi with salad and garlic bread 112

Indian marinated chicken salad 126

insalata caprese 102

lamb, capsicum and cucumber salad 127

minced pork and noodle salad 124

modern salad Niçoise 93

orange, goat's cheese and hazelnut salad 111

pear and walnut salad with lime vinaigrette 110

prawn, mango and macadamia salad 120

prawn and fennel salad 116

radicchio with figs and ginger vinaigrette 99

roast duck salad with chilli dressing 129

roast tomato salad 103

roasted tomato and bocconcini salad 117

scallop salad with saffron dressing 112

scallops, ginger and spinach salad 122

somen noodle salad with sesame dressing 118

spice-crusted salmon and noodle salad 80

spicy lamb and noodle salad 125

spinach salad with chicken and sesame dressing 133

tabbouleh 98

Thai marinated octopus salad 114

Tuscan bread salad 95

Vietnamese prawn salad 121

warm chicken and pasta salad 130

wild rice salad 119

salmon

    fresh salmon patties with mango salsa 43

    salmon with bean purée 66

    salmon fillets with lemon hollandaise sauce 48

    salmon kedgeree 49

    salmon with miso and soy noodles 54

    spice-crusted salmon and noodle salad 80

salt and pepper chicken with Asian greens 57

salt and pepper squid 40

saltimbocca 75

san choy bau, pork 26

sauces

    lemon mustard sauce 70

    pea sauce 82

sausages, spicy, with harissa and couscous 58

scallops

    scallop fritters 27

    scallop salad with saffron dressing 112

    scallops, ginger and spinach salad 122

seafood

    asparagus with smoked salmon and eggs 18

bagels with smoked salmon and caper salsa 37

chargrilled baby octopus 17

farfalle with prawns and horseradish cream 55

fresh salmon patties with mango salsa 43

john dory with prawns and creamy dill sauce 88

lemon pepper tuna burger 41

prawn, mango and macadamia salad 120

prawn cocktails 16

prawn and fennel salad 116

prawn pulao 51

salmon with bean purée 66

salmon kedgeree 49

salmon with miso and soy noodles 54

salt and pepper squid 40

scallop fritters 27

scallop salad with saffron dressing 112

scallops, ginger and spinach salad 122

seafood pasta 67

sesame-coated tuna with coriander salsa 69

Spanish omelette with smoked salmon 36

surf 'n' turf 70

Thai fried prawn balls with spicy salad 42

Thai marinated octopus salad 114

tuna steaks on coriander noodles 89

Vietnamese prawn salad 121

    see also fish

sesame-coated tuna with coriander salsa 69

skewers, chicken, with spicy chilli 46

smoked salmon

    asparagus with smoked salmon and eggs 18

    bagels with smoked salmon and caper salsa 37

    Spanish omelette with smoked salmon 36

somen noodle salad with sesame dressing 118

spaghetti carbonara 52

Spanish omelette with smoked salmon 36

spice-crusted salmon and noodle salad 80

spiced fruit salad 147

spicy lamb and noodle salad 125

spicy sausages with harissa and couscous 58

spinach with chicken and sesame dressing 133

spring rolls, fresh 20

squid, salt and pepper 40

steak with maître d'hotel butter 71

strawberries with balsamic vinegar 139

surf 'n' turf 70

sweet potato and leek frittatas, mini 22

T

tabbouleh 98

tapenade 12

Thai fried prawn balls with spicy salad 42

Thai marinated octopus salad 114

tiramisu 150

tofu

    Asian tofu salad 123

    grilled tofu salad with miso dressing 115

    tofu fajitas 38

tomatoes

    bruschetta 13

    Cajun chicken with tomato and corn salsa 87

    ciabatta breakfast toasts 19

    fresh tomato and basil sauce with pasta 53

    linguine with roasted cherry tomatoes 62

    quick pasta with tomato sauce 84

    roast tomato salad 103

    roasted tomato and bocconcini salad 117

trifle 157

tuna

    lemon pepper tuna burger 41

    sesame-coated tuna with coriander salsa 69

    tuna steaks on coriander noodles 89

Tuscan bread salad 95

tzatziki 11

V

veal

    saltimbocca 75

    vegetable and veal pasta 73

vegetable salad, chargrilled, with balsamic 96

vegetable strudels 15

vegetable and veal pasta 73

Vietnamese prawn salad 121

W

wild rice

    roast chicken with wild rice 50

    wild rice salad 119

Y

yoghurt

    lamb cutlets with spicy yoghurt sauce 59

    tzatziki 11

Z

zuppa inglese 151